the
blooming
platter
cookbook

the
blooming
platter
cookbook

A Harvest of Seasonal Vegan Recipes

Betsy DiJulio

VEGAN HERITAGE PRESS
Woodstock • Virginia

First Edition, May 2011

ISBN 13: 978-0-9800131-3-9
ISBN 10: 0-9800131-3-5

Vegan Heritage Press books are available at quantity discounts. For information, please visit the company website at www.veganheritagepress.com or write the publisher at Vegan Heritage Press, P.O. Box 628, Woodstock, VA 22664-0628.

Author Photo by Glen McClure Studio. Color insert photos by Betsy DiJulio.

Printed in Canada

Library of Congress Cataloging-in-Publication Data
DiJulio, Betsy.
    The blooming platter cookbook : a harvest of seasonal vegan recipes / Betsy DiJulio.
        p. cm.
    Includes index.
    ISBN-13: 978-0-9800131-3-9
    ISBN-10: 0-9800131-3-5
    1. Vegan cooking. 2. Seasonal cooking. 3. Cookbooks. I. Title.
    TX837.D47 2011
    641.5'636--dc22

Publisher's Note: The information in this book is true and complete to the best of our knowledge. Website addresses and contact information were correct at the time of publication. The publisher is not responsible for specific health or allergy needs that may require medical supervision, nor adverse reactions to recipes contained in this book. The author and publisher disclaim all liability in connection with the use of the book.

Dedication

For Mama, Dad, Ginny and Joe—

You Nourish Me.

Contents

Introduction

It is fair to say that long about high school, in the days before the Internet and T.V. food networks, I became obsessed with cooking. I devoured everything I could get my hands on: combing through and cataloguing a treasured set of culinary magazines deaccessioned by our local library, voraciously poring over cookbooks, studying and practicing methods and techniques, and experimenting on a very patient family. Erstwhile dreams of becoming a chef led me to a year of hotel and restaurant management courses in college.

Though I ultimately chose to pursue an academic and vocational direction in the visual arts, I have remained faithful to my other love. In college and after graduate school, I became smitten with catering and worked part-time for several years both for myself and various companies, including the award-winning Clean Plate Club in Nashville, TN owned by my friend Monica Holmes. Since then, I have been consumed by what I like to call intense "investigative" home-cooking and entertaining – fueled by the advent of the food networks – ultimately leading to part-time freelance food writing and a bit of teaching. I remain an "independent study" student of all things culinary.

Out with the Old, In with the New

Vegetarianism was my lifestyle choice for many years before I became vegan, and the journey was incremental. My decades exploring meatless cooking meant that, while I had come nowhere close to exhausting the possibilities, I was fairly well steeped in the vegetarian repertoire. As a vegetarian, I had been a "Dairy Queen," often creating royal feasts with butter, cream, sour cream, cream cheese, and cheese – lots of cheese. Anything tastes better – or so I erroneously thought – with dairy.

I remember the exact moment when I became a full-fledged vegan. It was in May 2006 at my annual all-girls Unbirthday Party. Talk around the dining table turned to my friend Sharon Tanner's then latest read, *The Omnivore's Dilemma* by Michael Pollan. As she summarized the book's central themes, I felt all my previous egg- and dairy-eating ways melt away. In fact, as she remembers it, I set my fork down saying, "Well, that does it." I got up from the table at the end of that meal a vegan, never once questioning my decision.

Two months later, I published an article entitled "Vegan 101" in the *Virginian-Pilot,* our local Norfolk, VA newspaper, eager to share the early results of my crash course in what was to me a new diet. Though I had been a freelance writer on topics of vegetarian food, home and garden design, and art since 2001, my emphasis now shifted to cooking without meat and dairy. Soon after, I was writing vegan features, a column, and teaching the occasional vegan cooking class.

As a new vegan, I did look back – there was far too much culinary history to simply forget – but mostly I looked forward, eager to begin my journey through what I would discover to be a lush new culinary landscape. My decision to adopt a vegan diet was not about depriving myself. Far from it! A lusty lover of food since childhood, I approached vegan cooking like any other.

For Everything There Is a Season

An unexpected bonus of my decision to adopt a vegan diet was a renewed sense of discovery in the kitchen. In March of 2009, I felt compelled to launch my vegan blog, The Blooming Platter (www.thebloomingplatter.blogspot.com), as a way of giving back to the vegan cooks who inspire me while also encouraging others to explore this exciting way of cooking.

As I developed recipes for my blog, and my book, I was determined to create deeply flavorful dishes that sing with the essences of the plant-based ingredients. In addition to acquiring a new appreciation for the flavors of the plant world, I discovered many new ingredients, such as my now revered nutritional yeast and vital wheat gluten. I became even more appreciative of the nutritional value of the food I was advocating to readers. And, because every recipe on my blog is accompanied by a photograph, I also became much more attuned to food's eye appeal.

It was with this in mind that I organized the chapters of my book, not only by type of dish, but by season. In a nation where "fresh" vegetables are available mostly year-round, we can't really fool Mother Nature. Veggies shipped around the country are picked sometimes weeks before they find their way to the supermarkets, so the conveniences have cost us our natural sense of seasonality. In the chapters of my book, I seek to rediscover the flavors, colors, and textures of what's fresh, season by season.

Welcome to The Blooming Platter Cookbook

As I wrote this book, seasonality, aesthetics, and nutrition joined taste and texture in the forefront of my mind. This growing consciousness on my part coincides with the "slow" food movement; a greater interest in fresh, local, and seasonal produce; and the resulting reinvigoration of farmer's stands, markets, and CSAs (Community Supported Agriculture) on both local and national levels.

And what do you know? It's no longer a secret that food that is more wholesome and beautiful to behold is also better tasting and more satisfying to procure, prepare, eat, and share. As you cook your way through *The Blooming Platter Cookbook,* I trust that you will discover the same.

Whether you are a vegan, a vegetarian, or simply someone who wants to infuse your diet with more good stuff from the earth, you will discover in this cornucopia of 150 recipes a celebration of nature's abundance that I hope you will return to again and again.

Blooming Basics

There is no love sincerer than the love of food. — George Bernard Shaw

Welcome...

Before taking any journey, culinary or otherwise, it is helpful to orient oneself, and that is what this chapter will do for you. It explains the order of the chapters and how to take advantage of the seasonal sections within them. You will also find information on a few essential ingredients, food preparation methods, and some helpful tools and equipment. Just as important, I offer encouragement and suggestions for maximizing your kitchen experience by making these recipes as they are or using them as starting points for your own creative interpretations.

Be Creative in Your Kitchen

For as long as I can remember, food has been the blaze that marked the path of my life. My mother, Sallie Gough, is an inspired and enthusiastic cook in her own right. She was a willing kitchen conspirator who welcomed me into her kitchen when I was barely old enough to clutch a spatula. We have spent many contented hours together there with Mama creatively supporting every dietary change I adopted along the way, encouraging my culinary experimentations, instigating many of them, and participating in still more.

My near lifetime of enthusiastic involvement with food meant that I knew my way around a kitchen reasonably well. In fact, the kitchen – anyone's kitchen – has always been one of my favorite places to be, whether I'm feeling happy, sad, expectant, or expansive. Long before I became an artist and art teacher, I sought out ways

to satisfy my irrepressible creative urges – and, okay, cravings and appetites – quickly discovering that there was no better place than the kitchen. After all, it takes a lot longer to make a masterpiece than to make dinner. So I've expended far more creative energy in the kitchen than in my studio.

Both artists and cooks start with a few simple tools and materials and transform them through a process that seems pure alchemy. That is not to say that you must be a certified creative person to produce culinary magic. Rather, the kitchen is a place where our eyes, noses, and taste buds coax from us creative tendencies that may have otherwise gone untapped.

Exercising our creativity for its own sake is one of life's greatest pleasures. All the better if we have a succulent stew or dessert to show for it in the end. By following the recipes in *The Blooming Platter Cookbook,* you will have plenty of both and much more.

These days I find that recipes have become a point of departure or background research for me rather than guides to be followed to the letter. I am far too fickle to commit myself to one version of most anything. (Is that the Gemini in me?) So I urge you to experiment and express your own passions through your personal take on each recipe. Let loose a little and experiment, as I tell my art students, with "purpose and intention." This is because, if I have learned anything about cooking, it is that palates are as individual as people themselves.

A Year of Living Deliciously

Month after month, farmers coax from the soil a succession of seasonal specialties so strongly associated with specific times of year that they have come to define them. But, of course, what is local and seasonal – and, hence, what is freshest and tastiest – depends on where you live. And, fortunately for us, many vegetables have two or more growing seasons depending on when they are planted.

The eight recipe chapters of this cookbook are organized in the traditional way, including Starters, Salads, Soups, Sandwiches, Main Dishes, Side Dishes, Desserts, and Brunch. Each chapter is divided into seasons identified by easily recognizable icons in the page corners, beginning with spring and ending with winter. These icons indicate recipes that are based on ingredients most strongly associated with the four seasons by most people in the U.S. For example, you will find recipes calling for crisp tart apples in fall, tender young asparagus in spring, hardy greens in winter, and plump juicy berries in summer. These divisions are part science and part custom, because they depend, of course, on the climate where you live. You can make any of the recipes any time of year if the vegetables are available at your local grocery store.

Icons of the Seasons

✽ Spring

✸ Summer

🍁 Fall

❄ Winter

You will find that many of my recipes serve up a twist on tradition. Rooted in regional American favorites, global cuisine, and my mother's kitchen, each dish celebrates the essential tastes, textures, and sheer beauty that only the freshest seasonal fruits, vegetables, and herbs bring to the table.

Ingredients, Methods, Tools, and Equipment

Following are a few notes on my preferences for ingredients, tools, and equipment; recommended methods and approaches; and helpful hints to keep in mind as you make my recipes.

Ingredients

Stock Options. When choosing to cook with vegetable stock over broth, it is helpful to know the difference: a stock is typically a darker, richer, and earthier foundation used in recipes. It is often more full-bodied than a vegetable broth. A broth tends to

Fresh Produce Through the Seasons

These days we can get many varieties of fresh produce all year long, whether they are seasonal to our location or not. At the same time, many vegetables have more than one growing season throughout the year. Still, certain fruits and vegetables are more closely associated with certain seasons than others. Here, then, is a list of produce (by no means exhaustive) arranged according to the four seasons as experienced by most people in the U.S.

Spring

artichokes
asparagus
avocados
chard
chinese cabbage
cucumbers
leeks
lettuces
mangoes

mushrooms
new potatoes
peas
radishes
rhubarb
shallots
snow peas
spinach
strawberries

Summer

apricots
basil
beets
bell peppers
berries
cherries
chiles
corn
cucumbers
eggplant
fennel
figs

green beans
leeks
lettuce
mangoes
melons
okra
peaches
plums
summer squash
tomatoes
watermelon

Fall

apples
bell peppers
broccoli
brussels sprouts
cabbage
cauliflower
celery root
chiles
cranberries
dates
fennel
grapes

greens, dark leafy
mushrooms
nuts
parsnips
pears
persimmons
pomegranates
pumpkins
shallots
spinach
winter squash
sweet potatoes

Winter

apples
avocados
beets
broccoli
brussels sprouts
cabbage
carrots
cauliflower
celery root
grapefruit

greens, dark leafy
mushrooms, wild
oranges
parsnips
pears
spinach
squash, winter (*e.g.* acorn, butternut)
sweet potatoes

have a lighter flavor than stock and is suitable for serving on its own. I prefer vegetable stock, but you may use either in your recipes.

The best tasting vegan stock is made from scratch. But, for the sake of convenience, I generally use a commercially prepared vegetable stock available in aseptic containers or cans. I also sometimes use vegetable bouillon cubes or vegetable base (powder or paste) which can be reconstituted with water to make a stock or broth. Vegetable base powders can additionally be used as a seasoning in soups, stews, sauces, and other recipes.

All of these products are typically available in well-stocked supermarkets, but an even wider selection can be had in specialty food stores and online. Regardless of where you purchase them, read the labels carefully if you want to monitor the sodium content or avoid ingredients such as monosodium glutamate (MSG).

In these recipes, use whatever vegetable stock or broth you prefer, either commercial or homemade – just be sure to taste as you cook and adjust seasonings accordingly.

Natural Sugar. My sugar of choice is natural sugar rather than refined white sugar. Though both are cane sugars, the former is less processed than the latter. Processing includes removing the molasses from the sugar juice by filtering it through a bed of activated carbon that may include bone char; vegans try to avoid white sugar for that reason.

Turbinado sugar, sometimes called raw sugar, is what is yielded after the first press-

Fresh, Frozen, or Canned?

Research on the nutritional value of fresh produce vs. frozen or canned vegetables is complex and depends on a number of variables. Though common wisdom asserts that fresh produce is better for us, we should keep in mind that even fresh produce loses significant nutritional value due to exposure to light and air when it is transported over long distances and stored for even a few days. Overcooking also diminishes the nutritional benefits of fresh produce.

Canned and frozen foods, on the other hand, are generally packaged immediately after harvesting, when the levels of nutrients are highest. A number of studies conclude that nutrients are not lost during canning and freezing as was previously assumed. However, canned and frozen fruits and veggies may contain higher levels of salt, sugar, and other additives, not to mention a less appetizing texture than their fresh counterparts.

There are other health issues to consider, namely the health of the environment, as vast resources are expended and pollutants/waste created in the processing, packaging, storing, and shipping of canned and frozen produce. Even fresh produce that is packaged and trucked from many miles away or grown using unsustainable practices, including the use of chemical fertilizers and pesticides, has a negative effect on the environment.

Hence, buying from local farmers – especially those using sustainable agricultural practices – and consuming fresh local produce, soon after harvesting and not overcooked, appears to be the healthiest choice for people, animals, and the environment we share.

ing of the sugar cane. Similar to turbinado is demerara, named after a colony in Guyana from which the sugar originally hailed. These natural and raw sugars are light brown in color with slightly larger crystals than refined white sugar, lending a pleasant crunch to foods. They also have a hint of molasses flavor. However, they are lower in moisture content than brown sugar, which is refined white sugar with molasses added back in during the processing.

Vegan Butter. Every cook probably has his or her favorite butter alternative. My staple vegan butter is a brand called Earth Balance®, available in both tubs and sticks at well-stocked supermarkets, making it easily accessible for most people. I use it because it has a good flavor and, whether in tub or stick form, bakes up beautifully.

Non-Dairy Milk. Non-dairy, plant-based milks or beverages are widely available and the options have grown to include almond, hemp, oat, and rice, along with the familiar soy. In addition to the flavors and consistencies of these milks, their nutritional make-up is complex and variable. Each has its pros and cons. While they all contain healthy fats, some are higher in calories and/or carbohydrates; some have natural occurrences of certain vitamins and minerals like calcium; some are fortified; and some contain nutrients that block the absorption of others. It is wise to conduct your own research and make your own choices based on your personal nutritional needs. Because approaches to processing and fortification change over time, continue to read labels. I prefer soy milk for its protein content, in addition to its flavor, body, and wide availability. For cooking, I almost exclusively choose unsweetened soy milk available at my local chain grocery store, though plain (or plain lite), with its slightly higher sugar content, is absolutely fine for non-savory dishes and desserts.

Methods

Selecting, Storing and Washing Produce. All of the recipes in this book assume that produce has been carefully chosen and properly stored, washed, trimmed, and peeled. You should select produce that is firm, not wilted or split, and free of blemishes, bruises, mold, mildew, off-odors, or discolored areas. Don't confuse "homely" with "blemished," because, for example, gnarled heirloom tomatoes are some of the best eats around. Once purchased, do not allow your produce to sit for extended periods in a hot place (such as your car) on a warm day.

Generally speaking, perishable produce – and it is virtually all perishable once picked – should be stored in the refrigerator and not washed until just before use, especially berries and mushrooms. Greens, on the other hand, may be washed, spun until thoroughly dry, and stored in a plastic bag in the refrigerator. Certain perishable fruits and vegetables such as avocados, citrus, garlic, melons, onions, and potatoes should be stored in a cool, dry place until cut. Once cut, they must be refrigerated. Uncut fresh tomatoes should be stored at room temperature for optimum flavor. Once cut, tomatoes must also be refrigerated.

All produce, organic or not, homegrown or purchased, including that which will be peeled, should be thoroughly washed and dried with a soft cloth or paper towel before cutting, cooking, or consuming. But avoid using soaps or detergents. Produce with firm or textured surfaces like carrots or cauliflower should be gently scrubbed with a vegetable brush. Mushrooms are an exception, as they are best wiped with a damp cloth rather than washed. If absolutely necessary, a very quick rinse, but never a soak, is acceptable. Before you wash the produce, wash your hands for at least 20 seconds with soap and warm water.

Toasting Nuts. Toasting nuts intensifies their flavor. When you toast nuts in a dry pan on the stovetop, it saves the energy of heating the oven. The stovetop method is particularly effective for small batches of nuts. Simply spread them in an even layer in a dry skillet over medium heat. As they toast, shake the pan or stir the nuts frequently, until lightly brown and fragrant, about 1 to 2 minutes, or slightly more depending on the size of the nuts. Remove the pan from the heat and pour the nuts into a bowl to cool, stirring occasionally as they will continue cooking until they have cooled down. It is best to chop nuts after toasting.

Getting the Most Out of Citrus Fruit

Juice yields vary depending on the fruit size, its moisture content, and the extraction method. To get the most juice, try this method: using your palm, roll the fruit on a work surface a few times, pop it in the microwave for 10 seconds, roll it again, and then slice it in half; either squeeze the fruit in your palm or use a hand-held juicer or reamer. Use a fine strainer to capture seeds and pulp. Generally, a large, thick-skinned lemon may have little juice, where a small thin-skinned lemon can have a lot. To get the maximum zest from the fruit skin, use a microplane grater (see below). Here are some general guidelines:

- 1 medium lemon = 2 to 3 tablespoons juice + 2 to 3 teaspoons zest
- 1 large lemon = about 1/4 cup juice + 4 teaspoons zest
- 1 medium lime = 2 tablespoons juice + 1 1/2 teaspoons zest
- 1 large lime = about 1/4 cup juice + 4 teaspoons zest
- 1 medium navel orange = 1/3 to 1/2 cup juice + 2 tablespoons zest

Equipment

Cast Iron Skillets. I am unapologetically old-school when it comes to most stovetop cooking, especially sautéing, indoor grilling, and shallow- or deep-frying, preferring my cast iron skillet to all other options. Since cast iron is heavy, you may prefer a skillet with handles on both sides of the pan to help with lifting. Well-seasoned cast iron is the original non-stick surface, comparing favorably to manufactured surfaces and surpassing other metals. An even distributor of heat, cast iron browns foods beautifully and maintains a steady temperature for frying. Plus, it is very inexpensive and durable to boot. It also transfers easily from stove to oven where it does not emit potentially harmful fumes, even at high temperatures. A porous metal, cast iron does require a simple seasoning process before the first use and periodically throughout the lifetime of the pan. Just follow your manufacturer's directions and be sure to dry it thoroughly after washing.

Microplane Grater. When I was just learning to cook, I avoided any recipe that called for citrus zest – or I would just omit it because zesting was such a chore. But the widespread availability of microplane graters in a variety of sizes, prices, styles, and blades (fine, medium, or coarse) makes this task, as well as the grating of chocolate, coconut, garlic, and ginger, a breeze. Often dishwasher safe, some of the graters also come with built-in blade covers for storage.

Silpat®. Say goodbye to cookies scorched on the bottom and stuck to your baking sheet. Silpat® is the brand name of time-saving non-stick silicone and fiberglass mats that replace parchment paper or oil for lining baking sheets in the preparation of baked goods, candies and confections. Flexible Silpat® sheets are available in a variety of sizes, make clean-up a snap, roll up for easy storage and, because they are reusable, reduce kitchen waste.

Seasons, Themes, and Variations

Variety is the spice of life and, hence, from time to time throughout this book, I have included variations to many recipes as a kind of "two for the price of one" bonus. Creating variations of favorite recipes is one of the most efficient, exciting, and gratifying ways to build one's culinary repertoire. But even when a specific variation is not offered, I encourage you to get those creative juices flowing and experiment by, say, making a fall recipe in winter and substituting similar produce and herbs appropriate for the season. Be sure to note your substitutions right in this book – all of my favorite cookbooks are annotated by hand in the margins – so that you can recreate your successes.

Seasonal Menus

Many of the dishes in virtually every chapter of this book are balanced enough to make a meal. But if you like the idea of multi-course dining, I offer these suggestions for dinner parties, holiday repasts, weeknight meals and lunches or brunches for every season of the year.

Spring

Dinner Party
Sassy Springtime Rolls (page 19)
Chinese Tempeh Lettuce Wraps (page 75)
Mango Coconut Cream Sorbet (page 151)

Holiday Celebration
Pasta with Broccoli, White Beans, and Sun-Dried Tomatoes (page 95)
Grilled Radishes and Spring Greens (page 40)
Chocolate-Covered Strawberry Tart (page 152)

Weeknight Meal
Knock-off-amole (page 22)
Caramelized Onion and Spinach Quesadillas (page 96)
Chocolate Carrot Cake (page 149)

Lunch or Brunch
Savory Bread Pudding (page 179)
Coffee Gelée with Strawberries and Crème Anglaise (page 150)

Summer

Dinner Party
Mediterranean Olive Rolls with Lemon Fig Dipping Sauce (page 26)
Tofu with Tomato-Caper Wine Sauce (page 105)
Quinoa and Edamame Pilaf with Red Chard (page 131)

Macadamia Shortbread Tart
with Lemon Mousse and Berries (page 156)

Holiday Celebration
Fried Cucumbers with Midsummer Mayo (page 25)
Big Easy Burgers (page 80)
Bourbon-Broiled Peaches (page 157)

Weeknight Meal
Zucchini-Stuffed Shells with Blooming Marinara Sauce (page 106)
Golden Caponata (page 24)
Lemon Verbena Shortbread Cookies (page 155)

Lunch or Brunch
Mediterranean Chickpea Pita Pockets (page 85)
Green Bean and Apricot Salad (page 46)
Cherry-Almond Clafouti Cake (page 154)

Fall

Dinner Party
Butternut Squash Bisque with Cranberry Gremolata (page 66)
Seitan with Broccoli and Mushrooms in
Creamy Tarragon Sauce (page 109)
Sweet Potato Layer Cake with
Butterscotch-Bourbon Cream (page 166)

Holiday Celebration
Pumpkin-Stuffed Shells with Sage Butter (page 112)
Caramelized Fennel and Figs (page 133)
Apple-Brandy Cake with Pecan-Praline Frosting (page 160)

Weeknight Meal
Moroccan Eggplant and Red Bell Pepper Salad (page 53)
"White Cheese" Pizza with Kale and Sun-Dried Tomatoes (page 115)
Cranberry Crumble with Rosemary-Pecan Steusel (page 163)

Lunch or Brunch
White Bean and Roasted Yellow Pepper Crostini (page 29)
Tunisian Couscous Salad with
Cumin-Pomegranate Vinaigrette (page 49)
Baked Apples Baklava with Cider Sauce (page 162)

Winter

Dinner Party
Sage-Scented Fettuccine with Butternut Squash (page 118)
Grilled Pear and Spinach Salad (page 54)
Chocolate-Orange Mousse (page 169)

Non-Traditional Holiday Celebration
Spicy Orange-Scented Sweet Potato Dip (page 36)
White Bean and Kale Stew (page 71)
Maple-Mustard Roasted Brussels Sprouts (page 142)
Pear-Rum Cupcakes with
Tea-Infused Butter Cream Frosting (page 172)

Weeknight Meal
Kung Pao Broccoli and Tofu (page 119)
Cinnamon Stick-Vanilla Bean Ice Cream (page 171)

Lunch or Brunch
Sloppy Tempeh Sandwiches with
Marinara Mushrooms and Spinach (page 91)
Orange-Espresso Chocolate Chip and Hazlenut Cookies (page 173)

In Good Taste

If one thing is certain, it is that there are as many different palates as there are people. Biological, psychological, and cultural reasons combine to account for why people prefer their food seasoned a certain way. Even familiarity and exposure play a role. Hence, the types and amounts of herbs and spices, including salt, used in cooking are highly individual preferences. So judicious tasting along the way as you prepare a dish is essential in order to be able to season food the way you like it. Remember that aroma and flavor are two sides of a coin and that makes achieving balance – however you define it – an important goal. Other than that, be creative, mix and match the seasons, and be fearless in putting your own spin on recipes.

The Blooming Platter Cookbook: A Harvest of Seasonal Vegan Recipes reflects my full-grown passion for conscious cuisine. It celebrates the earth's delicious, nutritious, and gorgeous gifts in every season. My sincere hope is that this book will become a pathway to new and richer kitchen experiences for you as you fuel your body, your spirit, and your own culinary creativity.

Starters

> "Civilization has taught us to eat with a fork, but even now, if nobody is around, we use our fingers."
>
> — Will Rogers

In the Beginning...

Indulge in some healthy noshing with these enticing dips, spreads, "cheeses," and more – all inspired by seasonal ingredients. These recipes are perfect for parties, although I often enjoy making a meal out of finger food. Welcome the spring with Fresh Pea and Tarragon Hummus or Sassy Springtime Rolls. Celebrate summer with tasty Fried Cucumbers served with delicious Mid-Summer Mayo. In the fall, enjoy Beet Muhummara, a jewel-toned spread that will make beet-lovers out of the most beet-averse. Warm up your winter with a beautiful, emerald-green Indian Saag Dip. With brilliant colors and delicious flavors, these tantalizing dishes are a great way to start a meal or enjoy by themselves.

Starters

red lentil-pistachio spread

Yield: 3 cups

I debuted this tasty recipe at a lovely Easter feast with friends. Surprisingly, it was the result of my accidentally overcooking the lentils. You gotta love those happy accidents. Variation: substitute toasted pumpkin seeds for the pistachios, if desired.

2 cups vegetable stock
2 bay leaves
1 cup red lentils
1 small red bell pepper, halved and seeded
1 cup finely chopped pistachio nuts
1 tablespoon walnut oil
3 tablespoons plain vegan yogurt

Pinch garlic powder
1 teaspoon minced fresh oregano or marjoram, or 1/4 teaspoon dried
Sea salt and freshly ground black pepper
Garnish: sprig of fresh oregano or marjoram or lemon zest (optional)
Accompaniments: pita or bagel chips, toast or crackers

1. In a 2-quart saucepan over medium-high heat, bring the vegetable stock and bay leaves to a boil. Add the lentils, stir well and reduce the heat to a simmer. Cook, stirring occasionally, for 10 minutes or until virtually all of the water has evaporated and the lentils are so tender that they begin to break down. Set aside and remove the bay leaves. Preheat the broiler.

2. Arrange the bell pepper, cut side down, on an oiled or foil-covered baking sheet and roast it under the broiler until the skin is blackened and blistered. Remove the baking sheet to a wire rack until the pepper is cool enough to handle. Peel off and discard the skin. Finely dice the flesh of the pepper.

3. In a bowl, combine the bell pepper, pistachios, walnut oil, yogurt, garlic powder, oregano, reserved lentils, and salt and pepper to taste. Mix well to combine. Transfer to a serving bowl, garnish as desired, and serve with your choice of accompaniment.

green bean pastry bundles

Yield: 4 to 6 servings

These bundles made with tender young green beans are so scrumptious that a dipping sauce seems a little like gilding the lily. If you want to dress them up, serve with a lemon vinaigrette.

1 tablespoon olive oil
2 large garlic cloves, minced
1 pound thin green beans, about 4
    inches long, trimmed

Sea salt
1/2 sheet Pepperidge Farm puff
    pastry, thawed

1. Preheat the oven to 400°F. Line a baking sheet with Silpat or parchment paper. Set aside.

2. Heat the oil in a large skillet over medium-high heat. Add the garlic and cook, stirring constantly for 30 seconds. Add the green beans and a generous pinch of salt. Stir fry the green beans for 3 minutes. Remove the skillet from the heat and transfer the beans to a bowl. Set aside to cool. Cut the puff pastry sheet into 12 strips, approximately 3/4 inch wide and cut each strip in half crosswise.

3. Working with 5 to 6 green beans at a time, make a bundle and hold it with one hand while you spiral the dough around it two or three times, beginning and ending with the ends of dough on the underneath side, gently stretching the dough if needed. Transfer the bundle to the prepared baking sheet and repeat with the remaining beans and pastry, positioning the bundles an inch apart. Bake for 15 minutes or until golden brown. Remove the baking sheet from oven and let the bundles cool for a few minutes before serving.

sassy springtime rolls

Yield: 8 spring rolls

This beautiful mélange of fresh spring vegetables, herbs, and tofu is light, refreshing, and pairs wonderfully with a deep red dipping sauce. I like to serve the sauce with small spoons so it can be ladled into the rolls after the first bite. This allows you to enjoy some peanuts in each mouthful.

Spring Rolls:
1 scallion, halved lengthwise and cut crosswise into quarters
1/2 bell pepper, any color, cut into 1/4-inch strips
1 carrot, cut into 1/4-inch strips
1 small yellow summer squash, cut into 1/4-inch strips
3 large radishes, halved lengthwise, then cut crosswise into paper thin slices
2 cups rice wine vinegar
1/4 cup natural sugar
3 large cloves garlic, halved lengthwise
1/2 teaspoon celery salt

1/2 teaspoon ground coriander
1/2 teaspoon ground ginger
Sea salt and freshly ground black pepper
14-ounces extra-firm tofu, cut into 1/2 x 2-inch strips
8 (8-inch) rice paper wrappers
16 baby spinach leaves
Fresh cilantro sprigs or Thai basil leaves

Dipping Sauce:
Reserved liquid from marinated veggies
1/4 cup vegan fish sauce
1 teaspoon soy sauce
2 tablespoons natural sugar
1/4 cup finely chopped peanuts

1. *Spring Rolls:* Combine the scallion, bell pepper, carrot, squash, and radish in a medium bowl. In a 2-quart saucepan over medium-high heat, combine the vinegar, sugar, garlic, celery salt, coriander, ginger, salt and pepper and bring to a boil, then pour over the vegetables and toss well. Cool to room temperature. Add the tofu, cover and chill overnight. When ready to use, drain the tofu and vegetables. Reserve the liquid to make the dipping sauce; remove and discard the garlic pieces.

2. Fill a large bowl half full with warm water. Place a kitchen towel beside it and a serving platter on the opposite side. Place one wrapper at a time into the warm water for 30 seconds or until softened. Remove from the water and place near one end of the towel. Fold the other end of the towel over the wrapper to blot excess moisture. Place two spinach leaves, face-down and overlapping, horizontally in the center of the wrapper. Arrange a piece of tofu horizontally in the center of the spinach and cover with 1/8 of the veggies, parallel to the tofu. Top with 1 or 2 cilantro sprigs. Fold the ends of the wrapper toward the filling, then fold the edge nearest you over the veggies and continue rolling. Place the roll on the serving platter, seam side down. Repeat with the remaining ingredients, changing out water if it becomes too cool.

3. *Dipping Sauce:* Whisk all ingredients except peanuts together. Divide the mixture among individual serving bowls, and top with peanuts. Serve with the spring rolls.

yvette's spiral bread

Yield: 24 slices

This bread is a signature dish of one of my best gal pals, Yvette Hetrick. The recipe is endlessly adaptable. Yvette fills it with creative combinations of savory ingredients, sometimes first slathering the dough with a thin layer of pesto. My spinach, onion, and bell pepper filling is delicious, but let it inspire your own made from seasonal ingredients with a similar moisture content.

Dough:
3 1/2 cups unbleached all-purpose flour
   (see note)
1 (1/4-ounce) package quick-rising
   yeast
1 tablespoon natural sugar
2 teaspoons sea salt, plus extra for sprinkling
2 tablespoons olive oil, plus extra for
   brushing
1 1/2 cups warm water, plus more if needed

Filling:
1 tablespoon olive oil
1 medium onion, chopped
2 medium cloves garlic, thinly sliced
1 large yellow, orange or red bell pepper,
   cut into 1/4-inch dice
8 ounces fresh mushrooms, chopped
6 ounces fresh spinach, stemmed
Sea salt and freshly ground black pepper

1. *Dough:* Preheat the oven to 250°F. Oil a baking sheet or line it with Silpat and set aside.

2. In a large bowl, stir together the flour, yeast, sugar, and salt with a fork. Make a well in the center, and add 2 tablespoons olive oil and 1 1/2 cups of warm water. Still using the fork, whisk together the wet and dry ingredients until the dough becomes difficult to stir. Add additional water, 1 tablespoon at a time, (up to 4 tablespoons, if needed), to make a soft, pliable, but not sticky, dough. Knead a couple of minutes. Turn off the oven and place the bowl inside for 10 minutes. Remove the bowl, punch down the dough and knead it another minute. Divide the dough in half. Cover and set aside.

3. *Filling:* Heat the oil in a large skillet over medium-high heat. Add the onion and sauté, until softened, 3 to 5 minutes. Add the garlic and sauté 1 minute. Add the bell pepper and continue sautéing until it begins to soften. Add the mushrooms and cook 3 to 5 minutes longer, then add the spinach and cook until wilted, 2 to 3 minutes. Season to taste with salt and pepper. Set aside.

4. *To assemble:* Working with one half of the dough on a lightly floured surface, leaving the other half covered, roll the dough into a 9 x 12-inch rectangle, 1/4 -inch thick. Spread with half of the filling, leaving a 1/2-inch margin. Starting on one long side, roll up the dough jellyroll fashion, then transfer to the baking sheet, seam side down.

5. Repeat with the other half of dough and filling. Transfer the second loaf onto the baking sheet, leaving several inches between the two loaves. Cover the loaves with a kitchen towel; return them to the still warm oven for 25 minutes. Remove from the oven and preheat the oven to 400°F. Return the loaves on the pan to the center rack of the oven. Bake for 25 minutes or until golden. During the last 2 to 3 minutes, brush the top of the loaves with olive oil and sprinkle with salt. Remove the pan to a wire rack and let the bread sit until it is cool enough to handle. Cut the loaves on a slight diagonal, into 1-inch thick slices. Serve warm or at room temperature.

Note: You can substitute 1 1/2 cups whole-wheat flour for the same amount of all-purpose flour.

fresh pea and tarragon hummus

Yield: 2 cups

May peas are transformed into a beautiful green hummus-like dish when combined with pistachios, olive oil, lemon juice, and fresh tarragon. The resulting spread is so tasty that a dinner guest once said she would have been happy to devour it with a spoon.

2 cups fresh raw green peas
1/3 cup shelled lightly salted pistachios
1/4 cup loosely packed fresh tarragon
  leaves
2 tablespoons walnut or olive oil
2 tablespoons fresh lemon juice

Sea salt and freshly ground black pepper
Garnish: chopped pistachios, a slice of
  lemon, or a sprig of fresh tarragon
Accompaniments: bread, toast, crackers
  or veggie dippers

In a saucepan, combine the peas with just enough water to cover. Place the lid on slightly ajar, and simmer over medium-high heat for 15 to 18 minutes or until tender. Reduce the heat if necessary. Drain and transfer to a food processor. Add the pistachios, tarragon, oil, lemon juice, and salt and pepper to taste. Pulse until desired consistency is reached. Check for seasoning, adding more lemon juice or salt and pepper if needed. Scrape the hummus into a serving bowl. Garnish as desired and serve with the accompaniments of your choice.

knock-off-amole

Yield: 3 cups

I developed a food sensitivity to avocados in my twenties. It was a sad day, as I was born in Texas and loved my mom's "guac." Even if you enjoy avocados, this dip is a delicious departure from the usual. If you like more heat, use an entire minced Serrano chile.

2 cups fresh shelled peas
1 tablespoon olive oil
2 tablespoons fresh lime juice
2 tablespoons nutritional yeast
1 cup grape tomatoes, quartered (use a serrated knife for easier slicing)
1/2 cup chopped red onion
1/4 cup minced fresh cilantro

1/2 small Serrano chile, split lengthwise, seeds and membrane removed, and minced
Sea salt and freshly ground black pepper
Optional garnish: a tortilla chip, fresh cilantro sprigs, or a wedge of lime
Accompaniment: purchased or Homemade Tortilla Chips below

1. Steam the peas in a steamer over a small amount of boiling water in a loosely covered 4-quart saucepan for 18 minutes or until tender. Drain well.

2. In a food processor, puree the peas with the olive oil, lime juice, and nutritional yeast until smooth. Scrape the mixture into a bowl and gently fold in the tomatoes, onion, cilantro, chile, and salt and pepper. Process until well combined. Taste and adjust the seasonings, if needed.

3. Serve garnished as desired accompanied by chips.

homemade tortilla chips

Yield: 24 chips

Canola oil
4 (6-inch) flour tortillas, cut into 6 triangles
Coarse sea salt

Heat a thin layer of canola oil in a large skillet over medium high heat until a drop of water sputters. Add the tortilla triangles and fry them for 1 to 2 minutes or until golden brown on one side; flip and repeat. Transfer to a paper towel to drain and lightly salt while still warm.

creamy summer torta with fresh figs

Yield: 8 to 12 servings

This simple layered appetizer is a favorite that I created during my vegetarian days using a combination of goat cheese and cream cheese. I do believe I like my vegan redux even better than the original. It is so beautiful and sumptuous with its contrasting earthy colors, flavors and textures. *Note:* Balsamic reduction is truly nectar of the gods, thick and tangy-sweet. If you are in a rush, plain balsamic vinegar is delicious too.

2/3 cup balsamic vinegar
14 ounces regular firm tofu, drained
2 cloves raw or roasted garlic (page 145)
2 tablespoons nutritional yeast, optional
2 teaspoons fresh lemon juice
1/2 teaspoon vegan Worcestershire
    sauce or Bragg Liquid Aminos
1/2 teaspoon sea salt
1/2 teaspoon seasoned salt

Freshly ground black pepper
Pinch natural sugar
1 tablespoon fresh rosemary leaves
2 teaspoons lemon zest
3/4 cup coarsely chopped fresh figs
1/2 cup coarsely chopped shelled salted
    pistachios
Garnish: 3 small fresh rosemary sprigs
Accompaniments: crackers or small toasts

1. Bring the balsamic vinegar to simmer in a small saucepan over medium-high heat. Reduce the heat to medium and simmer gently, uncovered, until it is reduced by half. Set aside.

2. In a food processor, combine the tofu, garlic, nutritional yeast, lemon juice, Worcestershire sauce, salt, seasoned salt, pepper, sugar, rosemary, and lemon zest. Process until smooth and creamy, scraping down sides as necessary. Scrape the mixture onto a serving plate or shallow serving dish and spread it to make an even layer about 3/4-inch thick.

3. Sprinkle evenly with figs, then pistachios. Drizzle with the balsamic reduction and garnish with rosemary. Serve immediately with the desired accompaniment or refrigerate, covered, until serving time. If not serving right away, wait until ready to serve before sprinkling with nuts and drizzling with the reduction.

golden caponata

Yield: 4 cups

Beautifully golden in color, this caponata's lusciously balanced flavors make a scrumptious appetizer on pita triangles, toast, or crackers. It is also delicious stuffed in a tomato, tossed with pasta, or spooned over grilled tofu or fried eggplant.

1 large onion, chopped
2 large cloves garlic, minced
1/3 cup yellow bell pepper, chopped
3/4 cup pitted green olives, minced
1 medium eggplant, unpeeled and cut
    into 1/4-inch dice
2 tablespoons olive oil
1/4 cup capers

3 tablespoons pine nuts
3/4 cup ketchup
1/3 cup water
2 tablespoons dry red wine
2 tablespoons natural sugar
1 teaspoon sea salt
1/2 teaspoon freshly ground black pepper
1/2 teaspoon dried oregano

1. In a 4-quart saucepan, combine the onion, garlic, bell pepper, olives, eggplant, and olive oil. Simmer, covered, for 10 minutes. Add the capers, pine nuts, ketchup, water, wine, sugar, salt, pepper, and oregano. Stir well. Simmer covered, stirring occasionally, for 25 minutes, or until the eggplant is tender.

2. Transfer to a bowl and serve with desired accompaniment. If not serving immediately, refrigerate until serving time, then bring to room temperature before serving.

trish's tangy tapenade

Yield: 3 cups

This chunky eggplant tapenade from my friend Trish Pfeifer makes a lot, but it keeps well in the refrigerator. And, it is so delicious you'll be glad you have extra on hand. Serve it as a topping for crostini for a quick-and-easy appetizer.

1 tablespoon olive oil
1 small eggplant, cut into 1/2-inch cubes
1 large ripe tomato, chopped
1/2 cup pitted and chopped Kalamata
    olives

1/3 cup toasted pine nuts
2 tablespoons capers
2 large cloves garlic, minced
1 tablespoon fresh lemon juice

Heat the oil in a large skillet over medium-high heat. Add the eggplant and cook, stirring, until tender, 10 to 12 minutes, reducing the heat if necessary. Remove from the heat and stir in the tomato, olives, pine nuts, capers, garlic, and lemon juice. Transfer to a bowl and use immediately, or cover and refrigerate overnight. Serve chilled or at room temperature.

fried cucumbers with midsummer mayo

Yield: 4 servings

This is my seasonal version of a favorite bar snack: fried dill pickles. If you don't have self-rising flour, you can make your own: combine 1 cup all-purpose flour with 1 1/2 teaspoons baking powder and 1/4 teaspoon salt.

Mid-Summer Mayo:
1 cup vegan mayonnaise
1/4 cup fresh sweet corn kernels
1/4 cup chopped ripe tomatoes

Cucumbers:
1 large English cucumber

Canola oil
1/3 cup plus 3/4 cup self-rising flour
Salt and freshly ground black pepper
3/4 cup plus 2 tablespoons light beer
Pinch garlic powder
Pinch onion powder
Paprika and fresh parsley sprigs, optional

1. *Mayo:* Combine all the ingredients in a bowl and stir gently to mix well. Set aside or cover and refrigerate until needed.

2. *Cucumbers:* Cut the cucumber into 1/4-inch slices on a steep diagonal. Drain on paper towel and pat dry. Heat a 1/4-inch layer of oil in a skillet over medium-high until a drop of water sizzles and sputters.

3. In a shallow bowl, combine the 1/3 cup of flour with a pinch of salt and pepper.

4. In another shallow bowl, whisk together the remaining 3/4 cup flour, beer, garlic powder, onion powder, and salt and pepper to taste. Add more flour or beer if needed to achieve the consistency of thin pancake batter.

5. Dredge the cucumber slices in the seasoned flour and then dip them in the batter before carefully lowering the slices, one at a time, into the hot oil. Fry six at a time for 2 minutes or until golden brown on one side. Carefully flip and fry 2 minutes on the other side until golden brown.

6. Transfer the fried cucumbers to a plate lined with paper towels. Garnish with paprika and parsley, if desired. Serve warm with the mayo.

mediterranean olive rolls
with lemon-fig dipping sauce

Yield: 30 pieces

These deliciously different rolls were a huge hit among an unlikely crowd: the muscle-bound guys at our gym's annual party. Seek out fresh figs for this recipe for their bright flavor and sparkling deep red color. Note: if figs are unavailable, substitute fig preserves and omit the sugar.

Olive Rolls:
1 tablespoon olive oil, plus more to brush the pastry
1/2 cup finely chopped onion
6 cloves garlic, minced
Sea salt and freshly ground black pepper
2 teaspoons fresh oregano leaves or 1 teaspoon dried
1 1/2 cups brine-cured pitted black and green olives
1/2 cup roasted and salted whole almonds
1 pound firm tofu, drained and pressed
2 teaspoons lemon zest
8 ounces phyllo dough, thawed (25 sheets)

Lemon-Fig Dipping Sauce:
1 tablespoon olive oil
1/2 cup finely chopped onion
3 cloves garlic, minced
Sea salt and freshly ground black pepper
1/2 cup loosely packed minced fresh dill weed
1/2 cup loosely packed minced fresh mint leaves
1 1/2 cups finely chopped fresh figs (or 11 ounces fig preserves)
1 tablespoon natural sugar
2 tablespoons red wine vinegar or balsamic vinegar
1/4 cup fresh lemon juice

1. *Olive Rolls:* Preheat the oven to 350°F. Heat the oil in a large skillet over medium-high heat. Add the onion and garlic and sauté until golden, 5 minutes. Season with salt and pepper, to taste. Reduce heat to medium, stir in the oregano, and cook it a minute to release flavor. Set aside.

2. In a food processor, combine the olives and almonds. Pulse to chop. Scrape the mixture into a medium-large mixing bowl. In the same food processor, combine the tofu, lemon zest, and salt and pepper to taste. Process until smooth and creamy. Scrape this mixture into the bowl with the olive and almond mixture. Add the onion mixture and stir with a spatula to combine the ingredients well. Adjust seasoning if necessary.

3. Remove the phyllo from its package and keep it covered with a damp cloth. Working with a stack of five sheets of dough at a time (for a total of five 5-sheet stacks), place the rectangular stack horizontally on your cutting board. Cut the rectangle in half vertically with a sharp knife. Spoon 3 tablespoons of the filling in the center of one of the halves and gently spread, leaving a 1-inch border all the way around. Fold the sides over the filling, creasing at the edge of the filling. Fold the bottom up over the filling in the same way and roll tightly. Repeat with the other half of the stacked dough.

4. Place both rolls, seam side down, on an oiled baking sheet. Repeat with the remaining dough and filling to make ten rolls. Brush them generously with olive oil and bake for 25 minutes or until golden. Remove the baking sheet from the oven, cool the rolls slightly and then remove them from the sheet to a wire rack. Cool them until barely warm.

5. *Lemon-Fig Dipping Sauce:* Heat the oil in a large skillet over medium-high heat. Add the onion and garlic and sauté until golden, 5 minutes. Season with salt and pepper, to taste. Reduce the heat to medium, stir in the dill and mint, and cook 1 minute to release the flavor. Stir in the figs, sugar, vinegar, and lemon juice. Cook 5 minutes or until the figs cook down, thicken slightly, and the flavors meld. Mash with a potato masher during the last minute of cooking. The sauce will be pulpy and slightly chunky. If you prefer a smoother sauce, transfer the mixture to a food processor and process until smooth. Transfer the sauce to a serving bowl.

6. *To Serve:* Cut each phyllo roll crosswise with a serrated knife into three pieces. Serve the rolls, warm or at room temperature, with the dipping sauce.

Note: In this recipe, I don't use the traditional method of oiling between the sheets of phyllo which, to me, takes too much time, uses too much oil, and isn't necessary.

beet muhummara

Yield: 4 cups

Inspired by muhummara, a Turkish spread typically made from roasted red peppers and walnuts, this stunning and addicting spread is perfect for festive occasions or any regular day of the week. Serve with warmed pita triangles.

3 large fresh beets, peeled and quartered (do not use canned beets)
1 1/3 cups toasted walnut pieces plus more for garnish (optional)
1/3 cup Panko bread crumbs
3 large garlic cloves
1 tablespoon ground cumin
1 1/2 teaspoons sea salt

Freshly ground black pepper
1/8 teaspoon red pepper flakes
2 tablespoons pomegranate molasses (page 36) or mild molasses, not blackstrap
3 tablespoons lemon juice
1/3 cup olive oil

In a food processor, combine the beets, walnuts, bread crumbs, garlic, cumin, salt, pepper, red pepper flakes, molasses, and lemon juice and pulse to a textured paste. With the motor running, drizzle in the olive oil and process until fairly smooth, but still textured. Scrape the mixture into a serving bowl, garnish with walnuts, if using, and serve.

seitan pâté with sautéed pears

Yield: 12 servings

The pâté was inspired by a recipe from my good friend Monica Holmes, owner of the award-winning Nashville catering company, The Clean Plate Club. My vegan version is rich and savory; the addition of the beautiful fresh pears provides a perfect contrast of flavors.

Pâté:
1 1/4 cup raw pecan pieces
1 tablespoon olive oil
1/2 large red onion, cut into 1/4-inch dice
3 cloves garlic, sliced
8 ounces baby portobello mushrooms,
      cut into 1/4-inch slices
1 teaspoon vegetable broth powder
1 teaspoon dried rosemary
1 teaspoon dried sage
1 teaspoon dried tarragon
1 teaspoon dried thyme
1 tablespoon vegan Worcestershire
      sauce, or Bragg Liquid Aminos
3 tablespoons cognac (or apple juice)

8 ounces seitan (page 117), cut into strips
4 tablespoons softened vegan butter
3 tablespoons unsweetened soy milk
Sea salt and freshly ground black pepper
2 tablespoons minced fresh parsley

Sautéed Pears:
4 tablespoons olive oil or vegan butter
4 ripe Anjou pears, sliced
2 to 4 tablespoons cognac (optional)
Pinch garlic powder
Pinch ground cinnamon
Sea salt and freshly ground black pepper
Accompaniments: Toasted baguette slices
      or pita chips

1. **Pâté:** Dry roast the pecans in a large skillet over medium heat, 5 to 7 minutes or until they take on a slightly toasted flavor. Transfer them to a bowl to cool.

2. Add the oil to the skillet and heat over medium-high heat. Add the onions and sauté them until they begin to soften. Add the garlic and sauté 1 minute. Add the mushrooms and sauté them until slightly softened. Stir in the vegetable broth powder, rosemary, sage, tarragon, and thyme and heat through. Add the vegan Worcestershire Sauce and cognac, sautéing 1 to 2 minutes or until the alcohol has cooked off. **Note:** Be careful, as alcohol can ignite, though the flames will extinguish when the alcohol has evaporated.

3. Transfer the mixture to a food processor. Add the pecans and seitan. Process until fairly smooth, scraping down the sides of the bowl a couple of times. Add the vegan butter and process for a few more seconds. With the motor running, stream in the soy milk until the mixture is smooth, scraping down the sides as needed. Season to taste with salt and pepper. Transfer the mixture into a serving bowl or onto a serving platter, smooth it out, and garnish with the parsley.

4. **Sautéed Pears:** In the same skillet in which the pâté was prepared, heat the oil over medium-high heat. Add the pears and sauté for 1 to 2 minutes, then add the co-

gnac, if using, along with the garlic powder and cinnamon. Sauté until the pears are slightly softened and golden, about 5 minutes. Season to taste with salt and pepper.

5. *To serve:* Serve slightly warm or at room temperature surrounded by sautéed pears with your choice of accompaniment.

white bean and roasted yellow pepper crostini

Yield: 4 to 6 servings

The pungent aroma of fresh rosemary and the zip of fresh lemon are the perfect complement to the earthy sweetness of this flavorful crostini topping. The topping mixture also makes a great dip or a spread for wrap sandwiches.

1 tablespoon olive oil
1 small onion, halved and thinly sliced
2 cloves garlic, minced
1 small yellow bell pepper
1 (15.5-ounce) can white beans, rinsed,
   drained, and coarsely mashed

8 oil-packed sun-dried tomatoes, drained
   and finely chopped
2 tablespoons fresh lemon juice
1 tablespoon minced fresh rosemary
Sea salt and freshly ground black pepper
Garnish: rosemary sprigs and lemon zest
1 small baguette, cut into 1/2-inch slices

1. Heat the oil in a large skillet over medium-high heat. Add the onion and cook, stirring, until lightly caramelized and golden, about 15 minutes. Reduce the heat to medium and add a small amount of additional oil or water to prevent sticking and scorching. Add the garlic, and continue to cook for 1 minute.

2. Preheat the broiler. Arrange the bell pepper, cut side down, on an oiled or foil-covered baking sheet and broil until the skin is blackened and blistered. Remove the baking sheet to a wire rack until pepper is cool enough to handle. Peel off and discard the skin. Finely chop the flesh of the pepper. Preheat the oven to 400°F.

3. Add the bell pepper to the onion mixture in the skillet. Stir in the white beans, sun-dried tomatoes, lemon juice, rosemary, and salt and pepper to taste. Keep warm.

4. Arrange the bread slices in a single layer on a baking sheet. Bake until golden brown, 6 to 8 minutes.

5. To serve, transfer the bean mixture into a serving bowl and garnish with rosemary sprigs and lemon zest and set aside. Serve warm, spread onto the toasted bread.

baked "brie" en croûte

Yield: 8 servings

Hot out of the oven, this dish is a glorious thing to behold. It tastes and smells divine. Will it fool anyone into thinking that it is true dairy brie? No, but it is so good that no one will care. Serve with the Sweet and Spicy Curried Pecans (page 31) or the Seasonal Fruit and Red Wine-Onion Jam (page 31), or both, for spectacular flavor and texture combinations.

14 ounces extra-firm tofu, pressed, drained and blotted dry
3/4 cup roasted cashews
6 tablespoons nutritional yeast
1 tablespoon miso
3 tablespoons beer or non-alcoholic beer
1 tablespoon fresh lemon juice
2 teaspoons onion powder

1/2 teaspoon sea salt
1/4 teaspoon garlic powder
1/8 teaspoon ground coriander
1 box Pepperidge Farm Puff Pastry, thawed
Optional Toppings:
Sweet and Spicy Curried Pecans (recipe follows)
Seasonal Fruit and Red Wine-Onion Jam (recipe follows)

1. Combine the tofu, cashews, nutritional yeast, miso, beer, lemon juice, onion powder, salt, garlic powder, and coriander in a food processor. Process until smooth, scraping down the sides of bowl as necessary. Line two soup bowls, approximately 5 inches in diameter, with plastic wrap and scrape half of the mixture into each one. Smooth the tops, fold the edges of the plastic wrap down to cover the surface. Top with a smaller bowl or plate and place a heavy can on top to weight it down. Refrigerate for 4 or more hours.

2. Preheat the oven to 400°F. Oil a baking sheet or line it with Silpat. Carefully unfold the puff pastry sheets and gently roll across the folds of each with a rolling pin to help seal. Remove the "brie" molds from the refrigerator and pull back the plastic wrap from the tops. Invert each mold into the center of one of the sheets of puff pastry and remove the plastic. Bring the corners of each puff pastry sheet to the center of its disk of cheese, pleating and folding to cover cheese completely and so that it will lie fairly flat.

3. Carefully flip each one over and place them a few inches apart on the prepared baking sheet. Coax each pastry pouch into a near perfect circle with the palms of your hands. Bake for 20 to 25 minutes or until they are golden brown and puffed. Remove the baking sheet from the oven, place it on a wire rack and cool for 1 to 2 minutes. Using a spatula, transfer each pastry wheel to a serving platter. With a serrated knife, slice into small wedges and serve topped with pecans or jam, if using.

sweet and spicy curried pecans

Yield: 3/4 cup

2 tablespoons olive oil
3/4 cup pecan halves or pieces
Sea salt
1/4 teaspoon curry powder
1/4 teaspoon coriander

Pinch garlic powder
Pinch chili powder
Red pepper flakes
1 tablespoon brown sugar
1 tablespoon water

Heat the oil in a large skillet over medium-high heat. Add the pecans and a bit of salt and begin to toast, stirring continuously to coat with oil and to prevent scorching. Lower the heat if necessary. Once the pecans are very lightly toasted, add the curry powder, coriander, garlic powder, chili powder, and red pepper flakes to taste. Stir, and toast the nuts for another minute or two. When the pecans are almost done, add the brown sugar and water. Stir and cook to thicken and coat. Remove the skillet from the heat and transfer the nuts to a bowl to stop the cooking.

seasonal fruit and red wine-onion jam

Yield: 1 1/2 cups

Add further flavor to this jam with a tiny pinch of ground cloves, cayenne, or a bit of minced rosemary, added in the last few minutes of cooking. This jam is also delicious without the fruit. Simply use 2 onions instead of 1 onion and 1 piece of fruit.

1 tablespoon olive oil
1 medium yellow onion, diced
1 pear, peach, or apple, halved, cored
    or pitted, and diced
Sea salt

1/2 cup water
4 tablespoons brown sugar
1/2 cup dry red wine (I use a Chianti)
2 tablespoons balsamic vinegar
1 tablespoon fresh lemon juice

Heat the oil in a large skillet over medium-high heat. Add the onion, fruit, and salt generously to help extract moisture. Cook, stirring frequently, until the onion and fruit begin to soften. Add the water, raise the heat just a little, and continue to stir frequently until the mixture becomes quite soft and most of the moisture has evaporated. Add the brown sugar, red wine, balsamic vinegar, and lemon juice, and resume cooking and stirring frequently until the onions and fruit are as pulpy as you desire and the moisture has evaporated. Check for flavor balance and adjust to suit your taste.

white bean and pesto tart

Yield: 8 servings

This elegant appetizer combines the humble white bean with a flavorful spinach pesto and fragrant caramelized onions. Add some colorful sundried tomatoes and bell peppers, and you have a feast for your senses.

1 tablespoon olive oil
1 medium yellow onion, halved, and cut into 1/4-inch slivers
1 to 2 large cloves garlic, peeled and coarsely chopped
Sea salt
1 sheet Pepperidge Farm Puff Pastry, thawed

1 (15.5-ounce) can white beans, rinsed and drained
1/4 cup plus 2 tablespoons Spinach Pesto (page 33)
6 oil-packed sun-dried tomatoes, drained and coarsely chopped
Garnishes: red bell pepper strips and rosemary sprigs

1. Heat the oil in a large skillet over medium heat. Add the onion, garlic, and a pinch of salt. Sauté for 20 minutes or until the onion is soft and golden brown. Stir in the white beans, pesto, and sun-dried tomatoes. Cook until heated through and the flavors are married. Preheat the oven to 400°F.

2. Oil a baking sheet or line it with Silpat and set aside. Carefully unfold the sheet of pastry onto the baking sheet. With a knife, gently score a line 1/2-inch from the edge of the crust all the way around, making sure not to cut all the way through the dough. Using a fork, generously but gently prick inside the scored line. Bake the shell for 15 to 20 minutes until golden brown and very puffed. Remove the crust from oven.

3. Use the back of a spoon to gently crush down the puffed area inside the scored lines leaving a raised 1/2-inch rim all the way around.

4. Spoon the bean mixture over crust, spreading to the inside edge of rim. Slide onto a cutting board and cut into 8 squares. Transfer to individual plates or serve right from the cutting board. Garnish as desired.

Note: If not using the crust immediately, remove from oven to a wire rack to cool, then, when ready to use, preheat the oven to 350°F., crush down puffed area and fill as described above. Before cutting, place tart in oven for 15 minutes or until heated through. The crust is best if used within 2 to 3 hours after baking.

Variation

Blooming Vegetable Tart: Cut the pastry into a large circle before baking; after baking, arrange roasted vegetables (asparagus, zucchini, bell pepper) and sliced cherry tomatoes in a decorative pattern on top and bake a few minutes longer.

spinach pesto

Yield: 1 1/2 cups

10 ounces fresh baby spinach, rinsed
   and dried
1 cup lightly packed fresh basil leaves,
   rinsed and dried
4 garlic cloves

1 cup lightly toasted walnut pieces
1 teaspoon nutritional yeast, optional
1/4 cup fresh lemon juice
1/2 teaspoon sea salt
1/3 cup olive oil

Place one-third of the spinach in a food processor. Process until finely chopped. Continue adding the remaining spinach, scraping down sides as necessary. Add the garlic, walnuts, nutritional yeast, if using, lemon juice, and salt, and process to combine. With the machine running, stream in the oil until well incorporated. Do not over-process.

blooming broccoli dip

Yield: 4 cups

This colorful and creamy-crunchy dip was inspired by my friend Bert Cake's signature potluck salad. It doubles deliciously as a pita pocket sandwich filling. My Blooming Platter Mayo is very light and flavorful, but, to save time, substitute Vegenaise or other store bought vegan mayo.

3 tablespoons olive oil
2 tablespoons apple cider vinegar
1 tablespoons maple syrup
1/4 teaspoon curry powder
Sea salt and freshly ground black pepper
3 cups small broccoli florets

1/2 cup chopped red or orange bell pepper (or a combination)
2/3 cup golden raisins
2 scallions, thinly sliced
1 recipe Blooming Platter Mayo (page 91) or Vegenaise
3 ounces smoked almonds, finely chopped

In a large bowl, combine the olive oil, vinegar, maple syrup, curry powder, and salt and pepper to taste. Whisk well to combine. Add the broccoli, bell peppers, raisins, and scallions and toss to mix well. Fold in the mayo, a few tablespoons at a time, until the desired consistency is reached. Reserve any leftover mayo. Refrigerate the broccoli mixture, covered, several hours or overnight. Fold in the almonds just before serving. Taste and adjust seasoning if necessary. Serve chilled.

sherried mushroom bruschetta

Yield: 4 to 6 servings

Earthy mushrooms and fragrant tarragon cozy up in this versatile bruschetta topping that can also be served as a canapé filling or a hot dip with crackers. For extra flavor, rub a sliced garlic clove on the toasted bread before topping with the mushroom mixture.

1 pound mushrooms (white, cremini, or shiitake)
1 tablespoon olive oil, plus more for brushing bread
3 large cloves garlic, minced
1/4 cup dry sherry wine
2 teaspoons vegan Worcestershire sauce, or Bragg Liquid Aminos
8 ounces firm silken tofu

2 rounded teaspoons miso paste (any kind)
2 tablespoons nutritional yeast, optional
1/4 teaspoon red pepper flakes
1/4 teaspoon ground nutmeg
1/2 cup loosely packed minced fresh tarragon leaves
Sea salt and freshly ground black pepper
2 teaspoons unbleached all-purpose flour
6 to 8 (1/2-inch thick) slices Italian bread

1. Finely mince the mushrooms in a food processor and set aside.

2. Heat the oil in a large skillet over medium-high heat. Add the reserved mushrooms, garlic, sherry, and Worcestershire sauce and sauté until the mushrooms release their moisture and most of it cooks off, 5 to 7 minutes. Remove the skillet from the heat and set aside.

3. In a food processor, combine the tofu, miso paste, nutritional yeast, if using, red pepper flakes, and nutmeg. Process until smooth. Add the tarragon and pulse to combine.

4. Scrape the mixture into the skillet with the mushrooms and return to medium-high heat. Cook, stirring, until the tofu mixture is incorporated into the mushrooms. Continue cooking, reducing the heat if necessary to prevent sticking, for 2 to 3 minutes or until the mixture thickens. Check for seasoning, and add salt and pepper to taste. Sprinkle with the flour, stir to combine, and continue stirring until the mixture thickens and the flour no longer tastes raw, 2 to 3 minutes. Keep warm.

5. Preheat the grill or broiler. Lightly brush the bread slices with oil and place on a hot grill or under the broiler until golden brown on both sides, turning once, 1 to 2 minutes per side. To serve, spoon the warm mushroom mixture onto the hot toasted bread slices.

indian saag dip

Yield: about 1 cup

This dip reinterprets one of my favorite entrees. The bright green color and heady aroma are a tribute to the glory that is fresh spinach.

6 ounces fresh spinach (tough stems removed)
1 medium onion, quartered
2 large cloves garlic
1 (1-inch) piece of ginger, peeled and halved
2 tablespoons water
2 tablespoons olive oil
1 teaspoon ground coriander
1/2 teaspoon ground cardamom
1/2 teaspoon ground cinnamon
1/2 teaspoon ground cumin
1/4 teaspoon turmeric
1/8 teaspoon cayenne pepper
1/2 teaspoon sea salt
Freshly ground black pepper
6 ounces extra-firm silken tofu
1 tablespoon unsweetened soy milk
1 tablespoon fresh lemon juice
Accompaniments: toast or crackers

1. In a food processor finely chop the spinach and transfer to a medium bowl. To the same food processor, add the onion, garlic, ginger, and water, and process to a paste.

2. Heat the olive oil in a large skillet over medium-high heat. Add the onion paste and cook, stirring frequently, for 5 to 7 minutes or until the paste begins to turn golden. Reduce the temperature to prevent the mixture from browning. Add the coriander, cardamom, cinnamon, cumin, turmeric, and cayenne and cook for 1 minute. Add the reserved spinach and the salt and pepper to the paste and cook for 2 minutes, scraping up any caramelized bits from the bottom of the skillet.

3. In the same food processor, combine the tofu and soy milk and process until creamy smooth, scraping down the sides as necessary. Add the tofu mixture to the mixture in the skillet and heat through, stirring constantly and continuing to scrape up any caramelized bits. Add the lemon juice, stir to combine well, and adjust seasoning. Transfer the dip to a bowl and serve hot or warm with desired accompaniments.

spicy orange-scented sweet potato dip

Yield: 2 cups

This beautiful dip with its rich golden color and creamy texture can also be used as a spread or side dish. Accompany with warmed pita bread, crackers, or sliced vegetables for dipping. **Note:** To bake the potato in the oven, pierce it with a fork, oil the skin lightly, and bake at 375°F. for 45 to 55 minutes until tender, or microwave for approximately 7 minutes on high.

1 tablespoon olive oil
1 medium yellow onion, halved and thinly sliced
Sea salt and freshly ground black pepper
2 large cloves garlic, thinly sliced
1 tablespoon fennel seeds
1 navel orange, peeled, pith removed, and separated into segments
1 large sweet potato, baked or microwaved until tender (see note)

6 ounces firm silken tofu
1 tablespoon vegan fish sauce or rice vinegar
1 teaspoon pomegranate molasses (see below) or maple syrup
1/4 teaspoon freshly grated ginger
12 fresh basil leaves (Thai, if available)
1/4 cup lightly salted roasted cashews
1/4 teaspoon ground chipotle chili powder
1/4 teaspoon ground coriander
1/4 teaspoon sweet paprika

1. Heat the oil in a large skillet over medium-high heat. Add the onion and sauté, 5 minutes or until it softens and begins to turn a golden color. Season with salt and pepper, to taste. Add the garlic and sauté 1 minute, stirring frequently, or until softened. Add the fennel seeds and cook, stirring frequently, for 30 seconds to release their fragrance. Add the orange segments and sauté for 2 minutes or until they start to break down. Reduce the heat if necessary.

2. Scrape the mixture into a food processor and add the sweet potato, tofu, vegan fish sauce, pomegranate molasses, ginger, basil leaves, cashews, chipotle chili powder, coriander, and sweet paprika. Pulse, scraping down the sides of the bowl as needed, until the mixture becomes creamy. Check for seasoning and add salt and pepper if needed. Transfer to a bowl and serve warm or at room temperature.

Pomegranate Molasses

Tangy and sweet, deep reddish-brown in color, and with a viscosity similar to maple syrup, pomegranate molasses (sometimes called pomegranate syrup) is made by extracting the juice from pomegranate seeds and boiling it down until much of the water is evaporated. Featured prominently in Middle Eastern cooking, it can be made from scratch, but is typically available bottled in Mediterranean or Middle Eastern markets.

Salads

> "To make a good salad is to be a brilliant diplomatist—the problem is entirely the same in both cases. To know exactly how much oil one must put with one's vinegar."
>
> — Oscar Wilde

In the Mix...

These colorful salads combine the best of seasonal ingredients with delectable dressings. The zesty mustard vinaigrette is perfect for mellow roasted cauliflower. Another favorite taste sensation is spring radishes, which are transformed into sweet nuggets with curried olive oil and a quick sear in a grill pan. In the heat of summer, enjoy my Southern Salad with Sweet Tea Dressing – a beautiful combination of chewy quinoa, fresh corn, peaches, and boiled peanuts. Roasting fiery jalapeños tames their heat, rendering them mellow and deeply-flavored counterpoints to sweet roasted carrots and garlic. Add a peanut dressing and you have a perfect Thai-inspired salad.

Salads

asparagus-orzo salad
with white bean sausage

Yield: 6 servings

Filling, yet refreshingly spring-like, this salad is perfect for an al fresco lunch. You'll need to make the White Bean Sausage (page 110) well in advance, however, and you only need one for this recipe. The remaining sausages may be refrigerated or frozen for another use. If pressed for time, you can omit the sausage or substitute a storebought link. (Tofurky Kielbasa is a good choice.)

Salad:
1 tablespoon olive oil
8 ounces regular or whole-wheat orzo
2 cups boiling water
Sea salt
1 tablespoon olive oil
1 small yellow onion, diced
2 cloves garlic, thinly sliced
1 large orange or red bell pepper, seeded, and diced
8 ounces thin asparagus spears, cut into 1-inch pieces

1 White Bean Sausage (page 110), sliced
Freshly ground black pepper
4 tablespoons toasted pine nuts, optional

Sage Vinaigrette:
3 tablespoons olive oil
1 tablespoon fresh lemon juice
8 fresh sage leaves, stacked, rolled tightly, and sliced thinly
Pinch garlic powder
Pinch sweet paprika
Pinch turmeric
Sea salt and freshly ground black pepper

1. *Salad:* In a 2-quart saucepan, heat 1 tablespoon of the oil over medium-high heat. Add the orzo and, stirring continually, cook for 2 minutes. Add the boiling water, cover with lid slightly ajar, reduce heat, and simmer until all of the liquid is absorbed, stirring occasionally, 8 to10 minutes. Transfer to a large bowl and fluff with a fork.

2. Heat the remaining 1 tablespoon olive oil in a large skillet over medium-high heat. Add the onion and garlic and sauté just until soft and barely golden. Add the bell pepper and sauté for 2 to 3 minutes or until slightly softened. Add the asparagus pieces and sauté just until asparagus is tender and bright green, about 2 minutes. Add the sausage after 1 minute. Transfer this mixture to the bowl with the orzo and season with salt and pepper. Sprinkle with pine nuts, if using. Set aside to cool.

3. *Sage Vinaigrette:* Combine all the ingredients in a small bowl, and whisk to blend. Taste and adjust the seasoning as desired.

4. *To serve:* Drizzle the dressing over the salad, tossing gently until well combined. Serve immediately or cover and chill. Bring to room temperature before serving.

grilled radishes and spring greens
with maple-curry vinaigrette

Yield: 4 servings

The often overlooked radish gets its due in this deliciously different salad.

Salad:
8 large red radishes, ends trimmed, and
    halved lengthwise
1 tablespoon olive oil
1/2 teaspoon curry powder
Pinch sea salt

Maple-Curry Vinaigrette:
1 tablespoon balsamic vinegar

3 tablespoons olive oil
1 tablespoon maple syrup
3/4 teaspoon curry powder
Pinch garlic powder
Pinch sea salt

To serve:
2 cups spring salad greens
1 tablespoon chopped roasted peanuts

1. *Salad:* Heat an oiled grill pan over medium-high heat. While the pan heats, prepare the radishes.

2. In a small bowl, whisk together the olive oil, curry powder, and salt. Taste and adjust seasoning if necessary. Add the radishes and toss to coat.

3. Arrange the radishes on the hot grill pan, cut-side down, placing them close together. Grill for 2 1/2 minutes, then turn 90 degrees and grill for 2 1/2 minutes more or until slightly caramelized with nice grill marks. Baste with the remaining curry-oil mixture.

4. Turn the radishes over and cook for another 2 1/2 minutes or until they develop grill marks, basting again. The radishes should be tender, but not soft. Transfer to a plate and allow to cool slightly.

5. *Maple-Curry Vinaigrette:* In a small bowl, whisk together the vinegar, olive oil, and maple syrup. Add the curry powder, garlic powder, and salt to taste, whisking well to combine.

6. *To serve:* Arrange the greens on 4 plates. Top each with 4 radish halves, drizzle each with one quarter of the dressing, and sprinkle evenly with the peanuts.

thai-inspired salad with a twist

Yield: 4 servings

I wondered what would happen if I roasted some home-grown jalapeños along with the carrots and garlic to use in a salad with Thai flavors. What happened was magic! Serve this salad at room temperature for optimum carrot color, as refrigerated carrots just don't have the same lovely complexion. Gloves are advised when working with hot chilies.

Salad:
2 tablespoons olive oil
3 to 4 carrots, cut diagonally into 1/4-
    inch thick slices (about 4 cups)
12 cloves garlic, halved lengthwise
Pinch sea salt
3 jalapeños, halved, seeded, and cut into
    1/8-inch strips then halved crosswise

Thai Peanut Dressing:
3 tablespoons vegan fish sauce
1 tablespoon chunky natural peanut butter
1 tablespoon fresh lime juice
1 tablespoon minced fresh cilantro
Pinch sea salt

1. *Salad:* Preheat the oven to 400°F. Spread the oil in a large roasting pan. Add the carrots and garlic and toss well to coat. Season with salt. Roast for 20 minutes, stirring after 10. Add the jalapeños, and roast for 10 minutes longer, stirring after 5 minutes. Check frequently to avoid scorching. Remove the pan from the oven and transfer the vegetables to a serving bowl. Add more salt to taste, if desired.

2. *Thai Peanut Dressing:* Whisk together all ingredients in a small bowl.

3. *To serve:* Combine the vegetables with the dressing in a bowl and toss to combine. Serve at room temperature or chill until serving time. Alternatively, this dish may be served hot as a side dish.

A Bite of Salad

When I was staging the grilled radish salad (page 40) to photograph, I came up with a fun serving suggestion. I arranged the spinach leaves in Asian soup spoons with flat bottoms. I nestled a radish in each one and drizzled the dressing over. It was really fun to eat. To make the portions come out right, I recommend 4 spoons per person.

cucumber and mushroom salad

Yield: 6 to 8 servings

This salad is juicy, crunchy, and refreshing. With its fresh garden herbs and cucumber cubes, it is as cooling to look at as it is to eat.

8 ounces shiitake mushroom caps, cut
 into 1/4-inch slices
1 cucumber, unpeeled if organic, cut
 into 1/2-inch dice
6 tablespoons walnut or olive oil

1/4 cup fresh lemon juice
1/3 cup minced fresh dill
1/4 cup minced fresh chives
1/4 cup minced fresh parsley
Sea salt and freshly ground black pepper

Combine the mushrooms and cucumber in a shallow bowl. In a small bowl, whisk together the oil and lemon juice and drizzle over the vegetables. Sprinkle with the herbs, and salt and pepper, to taste. Toss gently and check for seasoning. Cover and chill if not serving immediately. Serve chilled or at nearly room temperature.

beet salad
with horseradish-walnut vinaigrette

Yield: 4 servings

My husband and I host an annual Julia Child's Birthday Party. Our friend, Mike Tanner, arrived as an avowed beet-hater and left won over by this lovely dish. We agreed that Julia would be pleased that he gave beets another try in her honor. Walnut oil is especially good in this recipe, but olive oil is fine too. If champagne vinegar is unavailable, use apple cider vinegar.

2 tablespoons olive oil
1 clove garlic, minced
Sea salt
3 tablespoons walnut oil
1 tablespoon champagne vinegar
1 1/2 teaspoons prepared horseradish
   (not cream style)

Freshly ground black pepper
4 cups water
4 medium-size beets, trimmed
1/4 cup chopped toasted walnuts

1. Combine the olive oil, garlic, and a pinch of salt in a small bowl and set aside.

2. In a separate small bowl, combine the walnut oil, vinegar, horseradish, and salt and pepper to taste. Whisk until well blended and slightly emulsified. Set aside.

3. In a medium covered saucepan, bring the water and a pinch of salt to a boil over high heat. Add the beets, reduce the heat to a simmer, partially cover the saucepan, and cook for 30 minutes or until tender. Drain and set aside until cool enough to handle. Peel the beets with a paring knife (the peel should slip right off), cut in half, and place the beets cut-side down on a work surface. Slice the beets crosswise as thinly as possible.

4. Transfer the beet slices to a medium-size bowl, drizzle the dressing over them, and toss gently. Cover the bowl, and refrigerate for 2 hours to allow the flavors to marry.

5. When ready to serve, drizzle the beets with the reserved garlic oil and sprinkle with lightly toasted walnuts.

black bean and roasted corn salad

Yield: 6 servings

Nothing compares to the flavor of fresh summer corn right off the cob in this crowd-pleasing salad infused with the flavors of citrus and cumin. The spiced pecans are a delicious and crunchy topping, although regular toasted pecans may be used instead.

Sweet and Spicy Paprika Pecans:
1 tablespoon plus 1 teaspoon olive oil
1 cup pecan halves
1 tablespoon plus 1 teaspoon natural
    sugar
1/4 teaspoon hot or sweet paprika
Sea salt

Salad:
3 ears fresh corn
2 (15.5-ounce) cans black beans, rinsed
    and drained
2/3 cup chopped red onion
1 1/3 cups grape tomatoes, halved

2 navel oranges, zested (zest reserved)

Cumin-Citrus Vinaigrette:
1/3 cup olive oil
4 tablespoons rice vinegar
Zest from 2 navel oranges
1 teaspoon spicy chili sauce
2 cloves garlic
3/4 teaspoon ground cumin
1/4 cup fresh cilantro leaves
2 tablespoons fresh mint leaves
Sea salt and freshly ground black pepper

To serve:
4 loosely packed cups fresh baby spinach

1. *Pecans:* Preheat the oven to 350° F. Combine the oil and pecans in a large baking dish, stirring to coat. Sprinkle with the sugar, paprika, and salt to taste.

2. Place the pan in the oven and roast the nuts for approximately 10 minutes or until lightly toasted, stirring once or twice during the cooking time. If the pecans aren't sweet and spicy enough, add additional sugar, paprika, and salt once the nuts are removed from the oven but while they are still hot. Toss well and transfer to another container to stop the cooking. Allow the pecans to cool completely. Set aside.

3. *Salad:* Preheat the oven to 400° F. Rub the corn with olive oil, sprinkle with sea salt, and roast for 15 minutes or until just a few brown spots appear. Cut the corn off the cob and transfer to a large bowl. Peel the oranges and remove the pith, separate into sections, and slice each section in half crosswise. Add the black beans, tomatoes, and oranges to the bowl, and gently combine.

4. *Vinaigrette:* Combine all the ingredients in a food processor and process until well combined, scraping down sides of bowl as necessary.

5. *To serve:* Drizzle the salad with the vinaigrette and toss gently to combine. Serve the salad on a bed of baby spinach topped with the pecans.

green bean and apricot salad

Yield: 4 to 6 servings

This salad was inspired by an abundance of green beans found at my favorite outdoor market. The tempeh variation below adds substance to the dish without overwhelming the sweetness of fresh apricots.

2 cups fresh green beans, trimmed and halved

2 fresh apricots or peaches, cut into 1/2-inch dice

1 1/2 teaspoons sesame oil

3 tablespoons vegan fish sauce

Sea salt and freshly ground black pepper

1/2 cup lightly salted and roasted cashew halves

1. Steam the green beans until tender but still bright green, 5 to 7 minutes. Rinse under cold water, drain well, and transfer to a medium bowl. Add the apricots and set aside.

2. In a separate bowl, whisk together the sesame oil, vegan fish sauce, and salt and pepper to taste. Pour the dressing over the green bean mixture and toss gently. Set aside at room temperature to marinate for 20 minutes. Add the cashews to the salad and serve immediately.

Variation

Sauté nine strips of tempeh bacon in 2 teaspoons of oil over medium-high heat until browned. Set aside to cool, then cut into bite-sized pieces and add to the salad when ready to serve.

---

blackberry and corn salad

Yield: 6 to 8 servings

This dazzling salad is a celebration of all things summer. The blackberries exude a ruby red juice which joins beautifully with sweet corn, fresh tomatoes, and aromatic basil.

4 ears fresh corn, husks removed
1 pint fresh blackberries, rinsed and well
    drained
2 Roma tomatoes, cut into 1/4-inch dice
1/4 cup chopped red onion
1 clove garlic minced

2 tablespoons basil leaves, stacked, rolled
    tightly, and sliced thinly
Juice of 1 lime
1 teaspoon pomegranate molasses or
    maple syrup
Sea salt and freshly ground black pepper

1. Preheat the oven to 450° F. Rub the corn lightly with olive oil and arrange on a baking sheet. Roast for 20 minutes, turning halfway through. Roast a few minutes longer for more caramelization. Set the corn aside until cool enough to handle then slice the kernels off the cobs and transfer to a large bowl. Add the blackberries, tomato, onion, garlic, and basil. Set aside.

2. In a small bowl, whisk together the lime juice and pomegranate molasses. Drizzle over the vegetable mixture and toss lightly. Add salt and pepper to taste and toss gently one more time. Cover and allow the flavors to marry for 30 minutes, or refrigerate and remove from the refrigerator 30 minutes before serving time.

southern salad with sweet tea dressing

Yield: 4 to 6 servings

Salads don't get any tastier than this beautiful, summery Southern salad. Use farm-fresh produce, if available, because the taste of the salad is largely dependent on the flavor of the corn and peaches. Boiled peanuts add a distinctive and delicious flavor. For a formal touch, serve the salad in teacups. Garnish with a sprig of mint or parsley to complete the pretty picture.

Salad:
1 1/2 cups water
Pinch sea salt
1 cup quinoa
3/4 cup corn kernels (I like to grill or broil it and cut it off the cob)
3/4 cup diced fresh peaches
3/4 cup shelled boiled peanuts
3 scallions, thinly sliced
2 teaspoons lemon zest
1/4 cup loosely packed chopped Italian flat leaf parsley
1/4 cup loosely packed chopped mint
Sea salt and freshly ground black pepper

Sweet Tea Dressing:
1 tablespoon instant tea mix (powdered or granulated, not leaf tea)
2 tablespoons apple cider vinegar
3 tablespoons olive oil
1 large clove garlic, minced
1/2 teaspoon brown rice syrup
1/2 teaspoon fresh lemon juice

1. *Salad:* In a 2-quart saucepan, with the lid slightly ajar, bring the water, pinch of salt and quinoa to a gentle boil. Cook for 20 minutes or until all moisture is absorbed. Watch closely so that quinoa doesn't stick to the bottom of the pan. Transfer the quinoa to a salad bowl and set aside to cool to room temperature. Add the corn, peaches, boiled peanuts, scallions, lemon zest, parsley, mint, and pepper, and toss gently to combine.

2. *Sweet Tea Dressing:* In a small bowl, dissolve the instant tea mix in cider vinegar, whisking to combine. Heat the mixture for a few seconds in the microwave if necessary to help the tea dissolve. Whisk in the olive oil, garlic, brown rice syrup, and lemon juice. Pour the dressing onto the salad, and toss gently to combine.

Note: If boiled peanuts are unavailable, try this substitution. The taste and texture will be a little different, but still good: Combine 3/4 cup roasted peanuts and a pinch of salt in a bowl with enough hot water to cover. Cover and let soak for 8 hours or overnight.

thai rice noodle and plum salad

Yield: 6 to 8 servings

Inspired by the gift of tiny sweet plums from a friend, this cool, light, and refreshing Thai-inspired salad is a feast for the senses. If you don't have plums, substitute grape tomatoes for a slightly different – but still delicious – flavor.

Salad:
1 (6.75-ounce) package rice sticks or thin rice noodles
1 tablespoon canola oil
8 ounces shiitake mushroom caps cut into 1/4-inch slices
1/3 cup vegan fish sauce

Coconut-Lime Vinaigrette:
4 tablespoons canola oil
4 tablespoons rice vinegar
2 tablespoons lime juice
1 tablespoon soy sauce
1 tablespoon vegan fish sauce
1 tablespoon Cream of Coconut (such as Coco Lopez)

2 tablespoons minced fresh Thai basil leaves
1 tablespoon minced fresh cilantro leaves
Pinch ground ginger or fresh grated ginger
Sea salt and freshly ground black pepper

To Serve:
16 small purple plums, halved, pitted, and halved again (or 16 large grape tomatoes, quartered)
1 bunch scallions, white and green parts, thinly sliced
Optional Garnish: chopped roasted peanuts or cashews

1. **Salad:** Break the rice sticks or noodles into a heat-proof bowl. Heat to simmering enough water to cover them. Pour the water over the sticks or noodles and set aside for 10 minutes to soften; then drain, rinse them in cool water, and drain again. (Or follow package instructions for softening/cooking). While the noodles soften, heat the tablespoon of canola oil in a large skillet over medium-high heat. Add the mushrooms and sauté just until they begin to soften, 3 minutes. Add fish sauce, and simmer, still stirring occasionally, until most of the moisture has evaporated and mushrooms are tender.

2. **Coconut-Lime Vinaigrette:** Whisk all ingredients together in a large bowl. Set aside.

3. **To assemble:** Add the mushrooms to the bowl containing the dressing, along with the plums, scallions and reserved noodles. Toss the mixture well to coat. The dressing will tend to settle at the bottom, so toss before serving. If not serving immediately, store, covered, in the refrigerator, and toss occasionally to distribute the dressing up from the bottom. Garnish with nuts, if using.

tunisian couscous salad
with cumin-pomegranate vinaigrette

Yield: 4 servings

Ever since discovering pomegranate molasses in a local market, I can't get enough of its tangy sweetness. Combined with cumin, it lends a rich flavor to this Tunisian salad.

Salad:
2 teaspoons olive oil
1 cup Israeli couscous (sometimes called Pearl couscous)
2 cups boiling water
Pinch sea salt
1/2 cup chopped red onion
2 tablespoons fresh mint
8 brine-cured green olives, pitted, and finely diced
1 cup chopped cucumber
Pinch sea salt

4 tablespoons coarsely chopped roasted pistachios

Vinaigrette:
2 teaspoons fresh lemon juice
2 tablespoons olive oil
1 teaspoon ground cumin
2 teaspoons pomegranate molasses
Pinch natural sugar
Pinch sea salt

To Serve:
4 sprigs fresh mint

1. *Salad:* In a 1-quart saucepan, heat the olive oil over medium-high heat. Add the couscous and cook, stirring, for 1 minute. Add the water, cover loosely, and cook 7 minutes, stirring occasionally. Uncover and cook another 1 to 2 minutes, or until the moisture has evaporated. Turn off the heat, and add the onion and mint. Transfer the mixture to a medium size bowl and cool to room temperature. Gently fold in olives and cucumbers. Check for seasoning and add salt to taste.

2. *Vinaigrette:* In a small bowl, whisk together all ingredients.

3. *To serve:* Use an ice cream scoop to mound one-fourth of the couscous onto the center of a salad plate. Repeat with the remaining mixture. Surround each mound with an equal portion of cucumbers and sprinkle each with the pistachios, dividing evenly. Drizzle each salad with the vinaigrette, and garnish with a sprig of mint. Serve immediately.

grilled romaine hearts
with five-spice and lime-roasted cashews

Yield: 4 servings

This different and delicious salad is an amalgamation of three different restaurant dishes: a grilled Caesar from a local pub; a regular Caesar with addicting spicy cashews on top (the only part I could eat); and a dreamy Chinese mustard sauce served with a mound of haystack fried potatoes at the China Grill in Miami's South Beach.

Salad:
2 heads of romaine lettuce
Olive oil
Sea salt

Vinaigrette:
1 tablespoon tahini
1 tablespoon warm water
1 tablespoon rice wine vinegar
1 tablespoon lemon juice
2 tablespoons Chinese style prepared
   mustard

2 tablespoons light brown sugar

Cashews:
1 tablespoon olive oil
Juice and zest of 1/2 lime
1 tablespoon light brown sugar
1/2 teaspoon sea salt
1/4 teaspoon five-spice powder
1/8 teaspoon cayenne pepper
12 ounces roasted cashew pieces

1. *Salad:* Remove about 9 leaves from a large head of Romaine lettuce. Slice the Romaine hearts in half vertically. Rinse the Romaine hearts on the inside and outside and let water run down between the leaves vertically. Invert and shake out well. Pat dry and then leave to air dry. The lettuce should be completely dry before grilling.

2. Preheat an indoor or outdoor grill or grill pan. Brush the interior and exterior surfaces of each heart of Romaine half lightly with the olive oil and sprinkle with salt. Place the lettuce, cut side down, on the preheated grill. Grill until nice grill marks develop, 6 to 8 minutes. Watch closely, as the time may vary. Flip the lettuce hearts as soon as the cut side has grill marks, and repeat. Remove the Romaine halves to four serving plates, blotting any moisture away first, if necessary.

3. *Vinaigrette:* Combine all ingredients in a small bowl, whisking until smooth. If your tahini has been stored in the fridge, warm the liquids for 10 seconds or so in microwave to help the sesame paste break down when combined. Cover and refrigerate any leftovers.

4. *Cashews:* Line a baking sheet with a brown paper bag, waxed paper, or parchment paper. In a bowl, combine the lime juice and zest, brown sugar, salt, five spice powder, and cayenne. Heat the oil in a wok or large saucepan over medium high heat. Stir the mixture into the hot oil, being careful not to splatter, then add the cashews.

5. Roast and stir for 7 minutes, lowering heat if necessary, or until the nuts are caramelized and taste slightly roasted. Avoid scorching or you will have to throw out the whole batch. Spread the nuts immediately onto the prepared baking sheet to cool completely. Save the can or jar that your cashews came in to store remaining spiced cashews.

6. **To assemble:** Drizzle each Romaine half with 2 tablespoons of the vinaigrette and sprinkle with a few of the spicy cashews. Serve with a knife and fork.

french lentil salad
with champagne-dijon vinaigrette

Yield: 4 to 6 servings

This simple dish was inspired by a salad I enjoyed at a tiny bistro in Paris on my husband's and my twentieth wedding anniversary trip. It is especially delicious when made with crisp fall apples.

2 1/4 cups water
2 bay leaves
1 1/2 cups green lentils, picked over, rinsed, and drained
3 tablespoons olive oil (or 2 tablespoons olive oil + 1 tablespoon walnut oil)
1 tablespoon champagne vinegar or apple cider vinegar

1 1/2 teaspoons Dijon mustard
Sea salt and freshly ground black pepper
1 large apple (any variety)
1/3 cup chopped red onion
1 tablespoon snipped chives
3 tablespoons lemon juice

1. In a 2-quart covered saucepan over medium-high heat, bring water and bay leaves to a boil, reduce heat to a simmer. Stir in lentils and gently simmer, partially covered, for 30 minutes. Check at 10 minute intervals, as lentils are easy to overcook; they should be firm enough to hold their shape when tossed with the other ingredients. Add more hot water if necessary to prevent sticking or scorching.

2. While the lentils cook, make the vinaigrette. In a large serving bowl, combine the oil, vinegar, mustard, and salt and pepper to taste. Whisk until well blended and slightly emulsified. Set aside.

3. Halve the apple lengthwise, scoop out the core with a melon baller or spoon, arrange each half cut side down on a work surface, and cut into 1/8-inch thick slices. Then stack several slices together on their sides and cut them into 1/8-inch matchsticks. Add to the bowl with the dressing as you cut them, and stir gently to coat in order to prevent discoloration. Stir in the onion and chives.

4. When the lentils are cooked, drain, rinse with cool water to stop the cooking, and drain well. Remove the bay leaf. Stir the lentils into the dressing mixture. Season with salt and pepper, and add the lemon juice, 1 tablespoon at a time, to taste. Toss gently to combine. Taste and adjust the seasonings if needed. Cover and chill the salad several hours before serving to allow flavors to marry.

red beans and rice salad
with cajun vinaigrette

Yield: 8 servings

I grew up with the Big Easy an easy drive from my hometown. My parents' love of the city, especially its cuisine, was transferred to my sister and me early on. Served with a spicy Cajun dressing, this salad is an ode to our beloved NOLA. For an extra "lagniappe" top with a dollop of Creole Mayo (page 81).

6 tablespoons olive oil
2 tablespoons apple cider vinegar
2 teaspoons Creole mustard (or stone ground or yellow mustard)
1/2 teaspoon vegan Worcestershire sauce or Bragg Liquid Aminos
1/2 teaspoon liquid smoke
1 1/2 teaspoons Cajun seasoning (or to taste)
Sea salt and freshly ground black pepper

1 large bell pepper (any color), chopped
2 celery ribs, quartered lengthwise and thinly sliced
3 scallions, thinly sliced
1 (15.5-ounce) can red kidney beans, rinsed and drained
3 1/2 cups cooked brown or white rice
1 Spicy White Bean Sausage (page 110)
Creole Mayo (page 81), optional

1. In a large bowl, whisk together olive oil and vinegar. Whisk in mustard to emulsify. Then whisk in Worcestershire sauce, liquid smoke, Cajun seasoning, and salt and pepper to taste. Taste and adjust the seasonings, if needed.

2. Stir in the bell pepper, celery, and scallions until well coated. Add the beans and rice, stirring gently after each addition to distribute the dressing. Season with salt and pepper, to taste. Toss in the sliced sausage or arrange the slices over the top of the salad before serving. Allow flavors to marry for 30 minutes before serving, or cover and refrigerate, removing it from the refrigerator 30 minutes before serving time to lose the chill. Serve with the mayo, if using.

moroccan eggplant
and red bell pepper salad

Yield: 4 to 6 servings

Fresh eggplant and bell peppers create a wonderful combination of flavors and textures. Add a Moroccan-inspired dressing and you have a truly delicious dish. Make this for guests or a potluck – it's so good, you will want to share!

Salad:
1 tablespoon olive oil
1 pound eggplant, cut into 1 1/2-inch chunks
Sea salt and freshly ground black pepper
1 tablespoon canola oil, or more
1 small yellow or red onion, chopped
2 large cloves garlic, minced
1 large red bell pepper, cut into 1/2-inch dice

Dressing:
4 tablespoons extra-virgin olive oil

1 tablespoon fresh lemon juice
1 tablespoon balsamic or red wine vinegar
1 teaspoon pomegranate molasses or maple syrup
1/2 teaspoon ground cumin
1/4 teaspoon chipotle or other chili powder
1/4 teaspoon ground cinnamon
1/4 teaspoon sweet paprika
Pinch of sea salt
Freshly ground black pepper

To Serve:
4 tablespoons minced flat leaf parsley or cilantro

1. *Salad:* Heat the olive oil in a large skillet over medium-high heat. Add the eggplant and cook, stirring frequently but gently, for approximately 8 minutes until softened and golden. Eggplant absorbs a lot of oil, so you may need to add a little more oil to prevent sticking; stirring will help prevent sticking as well. Halfway through the cooking, add a couple of generous pinches of salt and pepper.

2. Add the canola oil, stir well, and add the onion. Cook, stirring frequently, for 2 minutes, reducing heat if necessary to prevent sticking. Add the garlic and bell pepper, and cook another 3 to 4 minutes until the vegetables are softened and the garlic develops a golden color. Transfer the mixture to a large bowl. Set aside to cool slightly.

3. *Dressing:* Whisk all of the ingredients together in a small bowl. Pour the dressing over the vegetable mixture and stir gently to distribute evenly. Cool completely and then cover and refrigerate.

4. *To Serve:* If time allows, bring the salad to room temperature before serving either in a bowl or on a platter garnished, if desired, with parsley and/or cilantro.

spicy grilled pear and spinach salad

Yield: 4 servings

If it is even possible to improve on a perfectly crisp raw pear, spicing and grilling it is surely one of the ways.

1 tablespoon balsamic vinegar
3 tablespoons walnut oil
Sea salt
1 tablespoon olive oil
1/2 teaspoon sweet paprika

1/4 teaspoon chipotle chili powder or
    other chili powder
2 large ripe pears, cored and sliced
2 cups stemmed spinach or baby spinach
1/4 cup toasted slivered almonds

1. In a small bowl, whisk together the vinegar, walnut oil, and a pinch of salt. Set aside. Heat an oiled grill pan over medium-high heat.

2. In a medium bowl, whisk together the olive oil, paprika, chili powder, and salt to taste. Add the pear slices and toss to coat well. Arrange the pear slices in a single layer in the grill pan and cook for 2 minutes, or until nice grill marks develop. Flip the pear slices over and cook 2 to 2 1/2 minutes longer. Transfer to a plate and arrange in a single layer.

3. To serve, divide the spinach among 4 salad plates, top with 3 pear slices, drizzle with the reserved vinaigrette and sprinkle with the toasted almonds.

roasted cauliflower salad
with mustard vinaigrette

Yield: 4 servings

In this delicious salad, zesty vinaigrette and fried capers set off the mellow roasted cauliflower to perfect advantage.

Cauliflower:
1 head cauliflower, trimmed
2 tablespoons olive oil
Sea salt

Vinaigrette:
1 tablespoon balsamic vinegar
3 tablespoons olive oil

3/4 teaspoon stone ground mustard
Pinch sea salt

Capers:
2 tablespoons drained capers
1 teaspoon olive oil

To serve:
2 cups salad greens

1. *Cauliflower:* Preheat the oven to 400°F. Lightly oil a baking sheet. Remove just enough of the core of the cauliflower so it stays intact when sliced. Cut the cauliflower into 1/2-inch slices. If any large florets break off, slice them the same way. For the larger slices, cut off any excess core, leaving enough to hold each slice together.

2. Arrange the cauliflower slices on the baking sheet, brush with olive oil, and sprinkle lightly with salt.

3. Roast 15 minutes, then remove the pan from the oven and carefully turn the slices over. Roast for 15 minutes longer. Check periodically, as you want some color to develop on each side, without scorching them.

4. *Vinaigrette:* In a small bowl, combine the vinegar, oil, mustard, and salt. Whisk until well blended. Set aside.

5. *Capers:* Spray a small skillet with a light coating of non-stick spray. Place the skillet over medium-high heat, add the capers, and cook for 3 to 5 minutes, or until the capers begin drying out, shaking the pan frequently. Using a wooden spoon, release any capers that stick to the bottom. Add 1 teaspoon of olive oil and continue cooking capers, shaking the pan for another 2 to 3 minutes. Remove the capers to a small bowl to cool.

6. *To serve:* Divide the greens among 4 salad plates, top with several slices of cauliflower, drizzle with 1/4 of the vinaigrette and top with fried capers.

cabbage, apple, and caraway salad

Yield: 4 servings

This salad was inspired by my friend Karen Eide and her horse Roxy. Karen and I were joking about recipes for Roxy and, while a dressed salad isn't appropriate for a horse, she was on my mind as I chose ingredients. This salad also gives a nod (or a neigh) to the flavors of Hungary.

Vinaigrette:
2 tablespoons olive oil
2 tablespoons fresh lemon juice
1/2 teaspoon curry powder
1/8 teaspoon sweet paprika
1/8 teaspoon garlic powder
Sea salt and freshly ground black pepper

Salad:
4 cups finely shredded cabbage, loosely packed
1 large red delicious apple, cored, halved, and thinly sliced
1/2 teaspoon caraway seeds
Sea salt and freshly ground black pepper

1. *Vinaigrette:* In a small bowl, combine the olive oil, lemon juice, curry powder, paprika, garlic powder, and salt and pepper to taste. Whisk to blend well. Set aside.

2. *Salad:* Combine the cabbage and apple slices in a serving bowl. Add the dressing, caraway seeds, and salt and pepper to taste. Toss gently until well combined. Taste and adjust seasonings.

orange salad with cumin vinaigrette

Yield: 4 servings

This light and beautiful salad is absolutely heady from the smoky aroma of cumin. It is inspired by a Portuguese clementine salad introduced to me by my friends Trish Pfeifer and Knox Garvin.

6 fresh clementines or fresh mandarin oranges, peeled and sectioned
3/4 cup pitted green olives, halved lengthwise and cut crosswise
1/2 cup minced red onion

2 tablespoons olive oil
1 teaspoon ground cumin
Sea salt and freshly ground black pepper
1 teaspoon natural sugar, optional

1. Combine the clementines, olives, and onion in a large bowl. Set aside.

2. In a small bowl, combine the olive oil, cumin, salt and pepper to taste, and sugar, if using. Whisk until blended.

3. Drizzle the dressing over the salad mixture and toss gently to coat. Taste and adjust the seasoning if needed. Transfer to a large platter and serve immediately.

Soups

> "Beautiful soup! Who cares for fish, game or any other dish? Who would not give all else for two pennyworth of beautiful soup?" — Lewis Carroll

Beautiful Soup...

What an ingenious creation is soup: a satisfying meal full of flavor and nutrition, all in a bowl. I especially enjoy the challenge of translating the flavors of a favorite dish into a soup. For example, I reinterpret spanakopita, the traditional Greek spinach and feta pie, into a flavorful soup. Topped with phyllo croutons, the soup retains the delectable "buttery" crunch of the original pie's crust but makes a lighter dish. The Indian Samosa Soup is a pleasantly spicy and spoonable version of the Indian restaurant appetizer, while the Springtime Pot Pie Soup is a satisfying but lighter rendition of its homespun inspiration.

Soups

springtime pot pie soup

Yield: 6 servings

This soup has all of the wholesome goodness of a pot pie lightened up for Spring with a flaky puff pastry "crust" served like croutons on top. Alternatively, pieces of baked pie crust also make wonderful "croutons" for this soup.

1 sheet Pepperidge Farm puff pastry, thawed
2 tablespoons canola oil, divided
3/4 cup chopped onion
1 cup chopped carrots
3/4 cup chopped celery
1 to 2 tablespoons nutritional yeast
4 tablespoons flour
4 cups vegetable stock
3 cups diced new potatoes (1 pound)
1 cup fresh green beans, trimmed and cut into bite-size pieces
1 cup fresh shelled peas
8 ounces seitan (page 116), chopped
2 tablespoons fresh minced tarragon or 2 teaspoons dried
Sea salt and freshly ground black pepper

1. Preheat the oven to 400°F. Roll out the pastry into a square on a work surface. Cut into 2-inch squares and arrange on the baking sheet. Bake 20 minutes or until golden brown. Set aside to cool.

2. Heat 1 tablespoon of the oil in a large pot over medium-high heat. Add the onion, carrot, and celery, and cook, stirring, until softened, 5 to 7 minutes.

3. In a small skillet, combine the nutritional yeast and flour, and cook until the color and aroma deepen.

4. Remove the pan from heat and stir the flour mixture into the vegetable mixture with the remaining 1 tablespoon oil, stirring until well combined. Add the stock a little at a time, stirring after each addition, until smooth. Bring to a simmer. Add the potatoes, green beans, and peas, and simmer 10 minutes or until the vegetables are tender. Stir in the seitan, and cook until heated through. Stir in the tarragon, and salt and pepper, to taste. Serve hot topped with the reserved croutons.

indian potato-pea samosa soup

Yield: 6 servings

I have been an ardent devotee of Indian cuisine since the first Indian restaurant opened in the 1980s in Nashville where I used to live. Samosas, triangular pouches of spicy potatoes and peas, are a simple but flavorful treat. Here, they take the form of a soup featuring delicious fresh spring peas.

1 tablespoon olive oil
1 small onion, chopped
1 large clove garlic, minced
3 cups vegetable stock, divided
1 large bay leaf
2 Russet potatoes, cut into large dice
1 cup unsweetened soy milk

1 teaspoon ground coriander
1 teaspoon ground cumin
1/4 teaspoon turmeric
1/4 teaspoon ground ginger
1 teaspoon minced jalapeño, optional
Sea salt and freshly ground black pepper
2 cups fresh shelled peas

1. Heat the oil in a 4 quart saucepan over medium-high heat. Add the onion and cook, stirring, until softened, about 5 minutes. Add the garlic, and cook 1 minute longer. Add 2 cups of the vegetable stock, bay leaf, and potatoes, and simmer, loosely covered, for 12 minutes or until the vegetables are tender. Remove the bay leaf.

2. Pour the vegetables and broth into a food processor and process until almost smooth, in batches if necessary. Avoid over-processing or the potatoes will become gummy.

3. Return the soup mixture to the saucepan, and add the remaining 1 cup vegetable stock, soy milk, coriander, cumin, turmeric, and ginger. Heat through, stirring occasionally. Add the jalapeño, if using, and season to taste with salt and pepper. Stir in the peas and simmer for 5 minutes or until tender. Taste and adjust seasonings, if needed. Serve hot.

spinach-tortilla soup

Yield: 6 servings

This soup is inspired by my Texas roots. Based on traditional tortilla soup, I add lots of fresh spinach for an infusion of nutrition. If fresh epazote is unavailable, you can omit it or substitute cilantro; the soup will still be delicious with a slightly different flavor.

1 small yellow onion, coarsely chopped
10 ounces fresh spinach, stemmed
3 tablespoons canola oil
8 corn tortillas, coarsely chopped
1 tablespoon minced fresh epazote or
    cilantro
Sea salt
1 cup fresh tomato puree (or 1 cup pe-
    tite diced canned tomatoes in juice)

1 tablespoon cumin
2 teaspoons ancho chili powder
1/2 teaspoon garlic powder
6 cups vegetable stock
Freshly ground black pepper
Optional Garnishes: vegan sour cream,
    toasted pumpkin seeds

1. Puree the onion in a food processor until smooth. Transfer to a small bowl and set aside. Add the spinach to the same food processor and coarsely chop. Set aside.

2. Heat the oil in a 4-quart saucepan over medium heat. Add the tortillas and epazote, and sauté until soft, 2 to 3 minutes. Season with salt to taste.

3. Increase the heat to medium-high, add the reserved onion puree and the tomatoes, and bring to a gentle boil. Add the cumin, chili powder, garlic powder, and stock and season to taste with salt and pepper. Reduce heat to a simmer and cook, stirring frequently, for 30 minutes. Just before serving, stir in the reserved spinach, and gently heat through. Serve hot, garnished as desired.

curried corn soup

Yield: 4 servings

Fresh, sweet summer corn kernels make this soup extra flavorful, although frozen may be substituted when fresh is unavailable. Though adding a touch of mustard may seem odd in a curried soup, many Indian recipes call for ground mustard powder or mustard seeds.

1 tablespoon olive oil
1 small yellow onion, diced
1 large clove garlic, minced
4 cups fresh or frozen corn kernels, divided
1 cup vegetable stock, divided
1 cup water

1/2 cup unsweetened soy milk
1 bay leaf
1 tablespoon curry powder
1/2 teaspoon prepared mustard
3 tablespoons minced fresh basil
Sea salt and freshly ground black pepper

1. Heat the oil in a large skillet over medium-high heat. Add the onion, and cook, stirring frequently until softened, about 5 minutes. Add the garlic and cook, stirring, until tender, about 1 minute longer. Remove the pan from the heat.

2. Transfer the onion mixture to a food processor, add 2 1/2 cups of corn kernels and 1/2 cup vegetable stock, and puree until smooth. Transfer the mixture to a 2-quart saucepan and add the remaining 1/2 cup vegetable stock, water, soy milk, bay leaf, the remaining 1 1/2 cups corn, curry powder, mustard, and basil. Season to taste with salt and pepper. Bring to a simmer and cook gently for 10 to 12 minutes, or until the flavors are well blended. Remove the bay leaf. Serve hot.

red pepper paprikash soup

Yield: 4 servings

This gorgeous red soup celebrates the first bell peppers of the season. The addition of sweet paprika makes it extra special.

1 large Russet potato, unpeeled, and
  halved
1 cup vegetable stock
1 cup water
1 bay leaf
2 large red bell peppers, cut lengthwise,
  and seeded

1/4 cup tomato paste
2 teaspoons ground sweet paprika
2 tablespoons dry red wine
Sea salt and freshly ground black pepper
Optional garnishes: vegan sour cream and
  fresh basil sprigs

1. Combine the potato with the stock, water, and bay leaf in a 2-quart saucepan, and simmer until tender, 10 to 15 minutes. Transfer the potato to a bowl until cool enough to handle. Reserve the cooking liquid in the saucepan. Remove the peel from potato halves and discard. Remove the bay leaf.

2. Preheat the broiler. Arrange the peppers, cut side down, on a baking sheet. Cut slits at both ends to help them lie flat. Place the baking sheet on the top shelf of your oven and broil until most of the skin becomes blistered and charred. Remove the baking sheet from the oven and set aside until the peppers are cool enough to handle. Peel off the skin and discard.

3. In a food processor, combine the peppers, tomato paste, paprika, wine, and salt and pepper to taste. Process until smooth. Stir the pureed pepper mixture into the warm potato soup base and heat until hot. Thin the soup, if desired, with additional stock. Taste and adjust the seasonings. Serve hot. Garnish with vegan sour cream and basil, if using.

snap bean stew

Yield: 4 servings

This stew was born in response to an over-abundance of sweet, locally-grown snap beans that a friend received in her CSA (Community Supported Agriculture) delivery and shared with me.

1 tablespoon olive oil
2 celery ribs, diced
2 carrots, diced
1 small onion, chopped
2 cloves garlic, finely chopped
Sea salt and freshly ground black pepper
2 cups snap beans, trimmed and cut
    into 1-inch pieces

1 tablespoon all-purpose flour
2 tablespoons nutritional yeast
3 cups vegetable stock
3/4 teaspoon minced fresh thyme or
    1/4 teaspoon dried
1/4 teaspoon minced fresh sage or a
    pinch dried

Heat the oil in a large skillet over medium-high heat. Add the celery, carrots, onion, and garlic, and sauté until softened, 5 minutes. Season to taste with salt and pepper. Add the beans and sauté for 2 to 3 minutes. Sprinkle evenly with flour and nutritional yeast, and cook, stirring, for 2 to 3 minutes so that the flour no longer tastes raw. Add the stock, thyme, and sage and cook 2 to 3 minutes longer, or until the beans are just tender, stirring frequently. Adjust the seasoning. Serve warm in soup bowls.

zucchini-hominy soup

Yield: 4 servings

I wasn't sure why I was craving this combination of ingredients one summer until after I created this soup. Then I knew. Not only do the flavors blend perfectly, but it is simple, nutritious, and beautiful to boot with its chunks of yellows, reds, and greens.

1 tablespoon olive oil
1 cup chopped onion
Sea salt and freshly ground black pepper
2 cups diced unpeeled zucchini (about 12 ounces)
1 tablespoon minced mild or hot green chile
1 tablespoon fresh minced oregano or 1 teaspoon dried

1 teaspoon ground cumin
2 tablespoons water
1 cup vegetable stock
1 (15-ounce) can petite diced tomatoes, undrained
1 (15-ounce) can golden hominy, rinsed and drained
Garnish: vegan sour cream and fresh cilantro sprigs

Heat the oil in a 4-quart saucepan over medium-high heat. Add the onion, and salt and pepper. Cook, stirring frequently, until tender and golden, 5 to 7 minutes. Add the zucchini, chile, oregano, cumin, and water, and sauté until the zucchini turns bright green and softens slightly, 5 minutes. Add the stock and tomatoes, and simmer 5 minutes. Add the hominy and simmer 5 minutes longer. Serve warm in soup bowls topped with vegan sour cream and cilantro.

butternut squash bisque
with cranberry gremolata

Yield: 4 servings

The zesty gremolata adds color, flavor, and crunch to this simple and familiar autumn soup.

1 tablespoon olive oil
1/2 cup chopped onion
1 clove garlic
1 small butternut squash, peeled and cut
    into 1-inch dice (about 3 cups)

2 1/2 cups vegetable stock
4 (4-inch) stalks fresh rosemary
2 bay leaves
Sea salt and freshly ground black pepper
Cranberry Gremolata (recipe follows)

1. Heat the oil in a large skillet over medium-high heat. Add the onion and sauté until softened, 3 to 5 minutes. Add the garlic and sauté until soft and slightly golden, 1 to 2 minutes. Add the squash, stock, rosemary, and bay leaves. Simmer, stirring occasionally, until the squash is tender, about 10 minutes. Remove and discard rosemary stalks and bay leaves.

2. Transfer the squash mixture to a food processor and process until almost smooth, scraping down the sides of the bowl as necessary. Return the puree to the skillet and heat through, stirring occasionally. Season the bisque to taste with salt and pepper, and serve warm topped with Cranberry Gremolata.

cranberry gremolata

Yield: about 1/2 cup

The gremolatas in this book are inspired by the traditonal Italian condiment, typically sprinkled on soups and stews and made with lemon zest, parsley, and garlic.

1/4 cup coarsely chopped walnuts or
    pecans
1/4 cup chopped fresh cranberries
1 teaspoon minced jalapeño

2 teaspoons fresh orange zest
Pinch sea salt
Pinch natural sugar

Combine all the ingredients in a small bowl and mix well.

caribbean black bean soup
with chili-nut butter

Yield: 4 servings

I've never met a black bean soup I didn't love. This one is ultra-thick with bright orange chunks of sweet potato that contrast beautifully with the jewel-like black beans. The Chili-Nut Butter and optional olive paste add little dabs of decadence that aren't absolutely necessary, but are absolutely fabulous.

1 tablespoon olive oil
1/2 cup chopped onion
1 clove garlic, minced
1/2 cup diced red bell pepper
2 cups vegetable stock
2 (15.5-ounce) cans black beans, rinsed
    and drained
1 teaspoon ground cumin
1 teaspoon ground coriander

1/4 teaspoon chipotle chili powder or
    other chili powder
1/4 teaspoon dried oregano
1 cup unsweetened coconut milk
1 medium sweet potato, cooked, peeled,
    and cut into 3/4-inch dice
2 tablespoons fresh lime juice
1 tablespoon olivada (page 145), optional
1 tablespoon minced fresh cilantro
Chili-Nut Butter (recipe follows)

Heat the oil in a large skillet, over medium-high heat. Add the onion and sauté until softened, 3 to 5 minutes. Add the garlic and sauté until the garlic is softened and golden, and onion has developed a little color, 1 to 2 minutes longer. Add the bell pepper and sauté until softened, 3 to 5 minutes. Add the stock, beans, cumin, coriander, chili powder, and oregano. Bring to a simmer, and cook 3 minutes, stirring occasionally, to heat through and allow flavors to marry. Stir in coconut milk and sweet potato and simmer until hot, about 5 minutes. Stir in lime juice, olive paste, if using, and cilantro. Simmer another minute. Serve hot in soup bowls topped with a small spoonful of Chili-Nut Butter.

chili-nut butter

Yield: about 1/4 cup

1 tablespoon vegan butter
1 teaspoon minced jalapeño
1/4 cup coarsely chopped toasted pe-
    cans or pumpkin seeds
Zest of 1 lime

Combine all the ingredients in a small bowl and mix well. Avoid over-mixing or the butter will melt. Serve using a small scoop or melon baller.

moroccan chickpea soup
with black olive-pumpkin seed gremolata

Yield: 6 servings

I love to find interesting ways to use pumpkin seeds, especially during the fall season. My pungent Black Olive-Pumpkin Seed Gremolata perfectly balances the silken creaminess and delicate sweetness of this flavorful soup.

1 tablespoon olive oil
1/2 cup chopped yellow onion
1 clove garlic, minced
1 (15.5-ounce) can chickpeas, drained
    and rinsed
1/2 cup pitted dates, cut into 1/4-inch dice
1 (15-ounce) can fire-roasted diced
    tomatoes, undrained
2 cups vegetable stock

2 teaspoons ground cumin
1 teaspoon ground coriander
1/2 teaspoon sweet paprika
1/4 teaspoon ground cinnamon
1/4 teaspoon ground ginger
1/4 teaspoon turmeric
2 tablespoons tahini
2 teaspoons fresh lemon juice
Black Olive-Pumpkin Seed Gremolata
    (recipe follows)

1. Heat the oil in a large soup pot over medium-high heat. Add the onion and sauté until softened, 5 minutes. Add the garlic, and continue to sauté until garlic softens and turns golden, about 1 minute.

2. Add the chickpeas and dates and heat through, stirring frequently. Stir in the tomatoes, stock, cumin, coriander, paprika, cinnamon, ginger, and turmeric. Simmer, stirring occasionally, for 15 minutes to allow flavors to blend.

3. Stir in the tahini until completely incorporated. It may look a little curdled initially, but keep stirring and it will smooth out beautifully. Stir in the lemon juice. Serve warm topped with Black Olive-Pumpkin Seed Gremolata.

black olive-pumpkin seed gremolata

Yield: about 1/2 cup

1/4 cup toasted pumpkin seeds
1/4 cup chopped pitted oil- or dry-cured
    black olives
2 teaspoons lemon zest

Combine all the ingredients in a small bowl, stirring to mix.

parsnip-cardamom soup
with hazelnuts

Yield: 4 servings

The delicious flavor of parsnips shines through beautifully when perfumed with ground cardamom, fresh ginger, lemon zest, and just a pinch of nutmeg. I love the way cardamom infuses savory dishes such as this with an enchanting flavor and aroma.

6 parsnips, cut into 1/2 inch disks
3/4 cup thinly sliced yellow onion
4 large cloves garlic, thinly sliced
1 (1 1/2-inch) piece of ginger, peeled
    and zested on a microplane grater
Sea salt and freshly ground black pepper
Unsweetened soy milk
3/4 cup dry white wine (I use a Pinot
    Grigio)
3 cups vegetable stock, divided

2 teaspoons ground cardamom
Pinch nutmeg
1 1/2 tablespoons olive oil
1 1/2 tablespoons vegan butter
1 1/2 tablespoons vegan sour cream or
    soy milk
Juice and zest of 1 lemon
1 tablespoon nutritional yeast, optional
2 tablespoons chopped toasted hazelnuts
2 tablespoons fresh minced parsley

1. Arrange the parsnips in a single layer in a large skillet. Sprinkle with onions, garlic, ginger, salt, and pepper. Add enough soy milk to just cover the vegetables. Bring the mixture to a simmer over medium-high heat. Cook for 15 minutes or until the parsnips are tender. Add the wine, 1/2 cup of the vegetable stock, cardamom, and nutmeg, and return to a simmer for 2 to 3 minutes.

2. Remove from the heat and transfer the mixture to a food processor. Process until smooth. Add the olive oil, butter, sour cream, lemon juice and zest, and nutritional yeast, if using. Process until smooth. Taste and adjust seasoning, if necessary. Scrape into a large saucepan, add the remaining cup of vegetable stock and heat through. To serve, ladle the soup into bowls and garnish with the hazelnuts and parsley. Serve hot.

mushroom and barley soup

Yield: 4 to 6 servings

As a child, one of my favorite winter soups was Campbell's Scotch Broth. I'm quite sure it was the satisfying barley that was responsible for my attraction.

1 tablespoon olive oil
1 yellow onion, cut into 1/4-inch dice
2 cloves garlic, thinly sliced
Pinch of sea salt
3/4 cup chopped celery
2 carrots, cut into 1/4-inch dice

8 ounces white mushrooms, sliced
6 cups vegetable stock
1 cup pearl barley
1/2 teaspoon dried thyme
1/2 teaspoon dried marjoram
1 bay leaf

1. Heat the oil in a 4-quart saucepan over medium-high heat. Add the onion and cook, stirring, until softened, 3 to 5 minutes. Add the garlic and a pinch of salt and cook for 1 minute. Add the celery and cook until it is softened, 2 to 3 minutes. Add the carrots, and cook 2 to 3 minutes longer. Add the mushrooms, and cook an additional 2 to 3 minutes.

2. Stir in the vegetable stock, barley, thyme, marjoram, and bay leaf. Cover loosely and simmer for 30 minutes. Add additional stock if the soup becomes too thick. Serve warm.

white bean and kale stew

Yield: 4 to 6 servings

This is such a warm and welcoming dinner to come home to on a cold winter day and it is especially good served with a loaf of crusty bread warmed in the oven. I like Lightlife's Gimme Lean® Ground Sausage Style in this stew, but another type of vegan sausage may be used instead. Sautéed tempeh or additional white beans may be used in place of the sausage.

1 tablespoon olive oil
1 yellow onion, cut into 1/4-inch dice
1 fennel bulb, cut into 1/4-inch dice
Sea salt
3 to 4 cloves garlic, thinly sliced
1 red bell pepper, cut into 1/4-inch dice
2 cups ground or chopped vegan sausage (see headnote)
2 bay leaves

Pinch dried basil
Pinch dried oregano
Pinch smoked or sweet paprika
1 tablespoon dried rubbed sage
4 cups vegetable stock
1 (15.5-ounce) can white beans, rinsed and drained
8 ounces kale, thick part of stems removed, and coarsely chopped

1. Heat the oil in a large skillet over medium-high heat. Add the onion, fennel, and a pinch of salt, and sauté until golden. Add the garlic and the red bell pepper and sauté, until softened, 3 minutes. Add the crumbled or chopped vegan sausage to the skillet. Sauté until the sausage develops a light golden brown crust.

2. Add the bay leaves, basil, oregano, paprika, and sage and stir well. Stir in the stock and white beans and bring to a simmer. Stir in the kale and cook for 5 minutes or until tender, but still bright green. Serve the stew hot or allow it to cool. Remove the bay leaves, cover, and refrigerate. Like most stews, this tastes best when reheated and served the next day.

spanakopita soup with phyllo croutons

Yield: 4 servings

Everyone's favorite Greek spinach pie – in a bowl! Crumble the buttery phyllo croutons on top for a quick preparation that has all of the flavor minus the labor.

Tofu "Feta":
7 ounces extra-firm tofu, pressed lightly
    and drained
2 tablespoons lemon juice
1 teaspoon dried dill weed
1 teaspoon dried mint
1 teaspoon dried oregano
1/2 teaspoon sea salt

Phyllo Croutons:
1/2 (8-ounce) package phyllo dough,
    thawed
2 tablespoons olive oil

Soup:
1 tablespoon olive oil
1 medium yellow onion, chopped
2 cloves garlic, thinly sliced
5 ounces fresh spinach, stemmed
1 tablespoon minced fresh dill
1 tablespoon minced fresh mint
1 tablespoon minced fresh oregano
3 cups vegetable stock
Sea salt and freshly ground black pepper
2 tablespoons fresh lemon juice

1. *Tofu "Feta":* Combine all ingredients in a small bowl and mash together until the mixture is well combined and resembles crumbled feta.

2. *Croutons:* Preheat the oven to 375° F. Leave the dough rolled like it comes in the package. Using a serrated knife, cut it into 1/2-inch wide strips. Pour 1 tablespoon of the olive oil into a medium bowl. Use your fingers to crumble the phyllo strips into the bowl. Drizzle with the remaining tablespoon of olive oil. Toss with your fingers until the dough is evenly coated in oil. Spread in a thin layer on a metal baking sheet. Bake for 7 to 9 minutes or until golden brown, stirring and spreading every 2 to 3 minutes. Remove the pan from the oven and allow the phyllo to cool slightly before using. Store in an airtight container at room temperature.

3. *Soup:* Heat the oil in a large skillet over medium high heat. Add the onion and sauté until it softens slightly, 5 minutes. Add the garlic and sauté until the onion is translucent and the garlic is softened. Add the spinach, dill, mint, and oregano, and sauté for 1 minute to warm through. Stir in the vegetable stock and simmer 8 to 10 minutes, stirring occasionally. Season to taste with salt and pepper. Stir in the lemon juice followed by the tofu "feta," and heat through. Serve immediately in soup bowls topped with the phyllo croutons.

Sandwiches

> "It has been well said that a hungry man is more interested in four sandwiches than four freedoms."
>
> — Henry Cabot Lodge, Jr.

Stacked, Wrapped, and Open-Faced...

You'll notice that the sandwiches in this chapter aren't your average PB&J. Many of them are special enough to serve company and hearty enough to enjoy for dinner. I love sandwiches of all types: open-faced, stacked, or wrapped. Some of the recipes include sub-recipes for complementary garnishes or specially flavored mayonnaise. If you're in a hurry, it's perfectly fine to use storebought vegan mayo and skip the extra garnishes. Whether you prefer to tackle your sandwiches hands-on, or favor the knife-and-fork variety, these flavorful combinations are bursting with savory seasonal goodness!

Sandwiches

chinese tempeh lettuce wraps

Yield: 4 servings

This Chinese-inspired tempeh "chicken" salad is made extra-refreshing by serving generous-sized scoops in fresh spring lettuce leaves. Allowing the salad to marry for a few hours enhances the flavor. This recipe makes eight good-sized wraps, but allow two per serving.

8 ounces tempeh, cut into 1 1/2-inch pieces
1 (8-ounce) can whole water chestnuts, drained
1 cup broccoli florets
3 scallions, cut into 1-inch pieces
1/2 cup baby carrots
1 cup lightly salted peanuts
1/2 cup lightly packed fresh parsley leaves

2 teaspoons five-spice powder
1 tablespoon nutritional yeast, optional
1 teaspoon vegetable broth powder
Sea salt
Garlic powder
Freshly ground black pepper
1/2 cup vegan mayonnaise
1 tablespoon soy sauce
Bibb lettuce leaves
4 tablespoons chopped peanuts, optional

1. Steam or simmer the tempeh for 10 minutes. Set aside to cool.

2. In a food processor, combine the water chestnuts, broccoli florets, scallions, baby carrots, and peanuts. Process until coarsely chopped, scraping down the sides of the bowl as needed. Add the tempeh, parsley, five-spice powder, nutritional yeast, if using, vegetable broth powder, salt, garlic powder, and pepper. Pulse until all the ingredients are finely chopped. Add the mayo and soy sauce and process until well mixed. Taste and adjust the seasoning, if necessary.

3. Make the wraps immediately, or transfer the tempeh mixture to a covered bowl and refrigerate until serving time. To assemble, spoon the mixture into the lettuce leaves, sprinkle with peanuts, if using, and roll up.

sesame-dusted portobello sandwiches

Yield: 4 sandwiches

Here, meaty portobellos are accented with the sweetly pungent flavor of Ginger-Carrot Relish and creamy Wasabi Mayo. For best flavor, make the relish and mayo ahead of time and refrigerate until needed.

Portobellos:
2 tablespoons olive oil
2 tablespoons toasted sesame oil
1 clove garlic, quartered
4 portobello mushroom caps
1 tablespoon sesame seeds

Ginger-Carrot Relish:
1 teaspoon toasted sesame oil
1 teaspoon soy sauce
1 teaspoon rice vinegar
Pinch sea salt
Pinch natural sugar
1/4 teaspoon grated ginger

1/8 teaspoon lemon zest
1 cup coarsely grated carrot

Wasabi Mayo:
1 teaspoon soy sauce
2 teaspoons wasabi powder
4 tablespoons vegan mayonnaise
1 teaspoon sake, optional
Pinch natural sugar
Pinch sea salt

To assemble:
4 whole grain buns, halved and toasted
8 grilled scallions, optional (page 77)

1. *Portobellos:* Combine both oils and the garlic in a small bowl and set aside. Preheat the oven to 350°F. Arrange the mushroom caps on an oiled or Silpat-lined baking sheet, gill-side up, and brush them lightly with half of the oil. Bake 12 to 15 minutes, or until they soften and release some of their juice. Flip the caps over, brush with remaining oil, and press 1/4 of the sesame seeds onto the top of each cap. Bake 10 minutes longer or until tender.

2. *Ginger-Carrot Relish:* In a small bowl, whisk together all the ingredients except the carrots. Add the carrots and toss gently to coat. Cover and refrigerate.

3. *Wasabi Mayo:* In a small bowl, whisk together soy sauce and wasabi powder. Add the mayo and whisk to combine. Whisk in the sake, if using, and the sugar. Season with salt, if needed. Cover and refrigerate.

4. *To assemble:* Spread the bottoms of each bun with a thin layer of the mayo. Top with a mushroom cap, sesame seed side up. Place a mound of the ginger-carrot relish on each of the mushrooms. Top each with a dollop of the mayo. Serve the sandwiches open faced, accompanied by the grilled scallions, if using.

thai seitan lettuce wraps

Yield: 4 servings

These wraps are bursting with luscious Thai ingredients. Enjoy a scoop in lettuce leaves for "roll your own" lettuce wraps. For heartier sandwiches, the seitan mixture is also great in tortilla wraps, stuffed into pitas, or enjoyed on toasted bread.

1 small red bell pepper, cut into chunks
1 cup baby carrots
3 scallions, cut into 1-inch pieces
1/2 cup dried pineapple pieces
1 cup lightly salted cashew pieces
8 ounces seitan coarsely chopped
1/2 cup lightly packed fresh cilantro
    leaves

2 teaspoons curry powder
1 tablespoon nutritional yeast, optional
1 teaspoon vegetable broth powder
Sea salt and freshly ground black pepper
1/2 cup vegan mayonnaise
1 tablespoon vegan fish sauce
Juice of 1 lime
8 Bibb lettuce leaves

1. Combine the bell pepper, carrots, scallions, dried pineapple, and cashews in a food processor. Pulse until coarsely chopped, scraping down sides of bowl as needed. Add the seitan, cilantro, curry powder, nutritional yeast, if using, vegetable broth powder, and salt and pepper to taste. Continue pulsing, scraping down sides as necessary, until finely chopped. Add the mayo, vegan fish sauce, and lime juice and process until the mixture comes together. Taste and adjust the seasoning and pulse a few more times to combine.

2. Serve immediately by scooping 1/2 cup of the seitan mixture into the center of each lettuce leaf and roll up. If not serving immediately, transfer to a covered bowl or airtight container and refrigerate until needed. Allowing the ingredients to marry for a few hours improves the flavor.

Grilled Scallions

For a delicious sandwich accompaniment, cut 8 trimmed scallions in half and arrange them on a grill pan. Grill a couple of minutes on each side until nice grill marks appear and the scallions are slightly wilted. These are especially good served with the Sesame-Dusted Portobello Sandwiches on page 76.

The Big Burgers of Summer

The Big Burgers of Summer recipes boast exciting combinations of spicy patties, juicy toppings, and creamy mayonnaises bursting with flavor. In addition to being delicious in a toasted bun with all the trimmings, these burgers are also terrific served as open-faced sandwiches eaten with a knife and fork. Chill the patties before cooking to help them firm up.

big kahuna burgers

Yield: 4 servings

Juicy grilled and slightly caramelized fresh pineapple rings top this burger which is but a nod – albeit a tasty one – to the complex American and Pan-Asian culinary influences of Hawaii.

3 large cloves garlic, crushed
1/3 cup coarsely chopped bell pepper
1/3 cup coarsely chopped onion
1/3 cup cashews or macadamias
1 (15.5-ounce) can black beans, rinsed
and drained
1/2 cup old-fashioned oats
1/2 cup vital wheat gluten
1 teaspoon lime juice
1 teaspoon soy sauce
1 teaspoon curry powder

1/2 teaspoon five-spice powder
1/4 teaspoon ground coriander
1/8 teaspoon cayenne pepper
1/2 teaspoon sea salt
1/4 teaspoon freshly ground black pepper
Canola Oil
4 whole grain buns, toasted
Big Island Mayo (recipe follows) or Vegenaise, optional
1 cup mixed salad greens
Grilled Pineapple Rings (recipe follows)

1. In a food processor, combine the garlic, bell pepper, onion, and cashews. Pulse to mince. Add the beans, oats, vital wheat gluten, lime juice, soy sauce, curry powder, five-spice powder, coriander, cayenne, salt, and pepper. Process until well combined. Shape the mixture into 4 patties, about 3/4-inch thick.

2. Heat a thin layer of canola oil in a large skillet over medium-high heat. Add the patties and cook for 5 minutes or until nicely browned. Use a spatula to turn the burgers and cook for 5 minutes on the other side.

3. On the bottom bun halves, spread 1 tablespoon of the mayo, if using, and top with a small handful of mixed greens. Add the patties, another tablespoon of the mayo, if using, and a grilled pineapple ring. Serve immediately with the top bun halves propped against the burgers.

big island mayo

Yield: about 1/2 cup

1/2 cup vegan mayonnaise
1 tablespoon lime juice
2 teaspoons brown rice syrup
1 teaspoon Cream of Coconut (Coco
    Lopez is a common brand)
Dash vegan Worcestershire sauce or
    Bragg Liquid Aminos
1/4 teaspoon soy sauce

2 tablespoons minced cilantro
2 teaspoons flaked coconut
1 clove roasted garlic, minced
1/2 teaspoon finely minced jalapeño
Pinch natural sugar
Sea salt
White pepper

Combine all the ingredients in a small bowl. Set aside or cover and refrigerate until needed.

grilled pineapple rings

Yield: Makes 4

4 (1/4-inch thick) slices fresh pineapple,
    blotted dry
1 teaspoon soy sauce
1 teaspoon lime juice
Pinch sea salt
Pinch natural sugar

Heat a well-oiled grill pan over medium-high heat. Brush one side of the pineapple slices with half of the soy sauce and half of the lime juice and place sauce-side down into the grill pan. Grill for 2 to 3 minutes, or until nice grill marks develop. Flip, brush with the remaining soy sauce and lime juice and a pinch of salt and sugar. Grill for 2 to 3 more minutes, or until nice grill marks develop.

big easy burgers

Yield: 4 servings

I was weaned on New Orleans and it remains one of my favorite cities in the world. Of course, the cuisine has more than a little to do with my passion for the Crescent City. This burger combines several favorite influences, from the red beans and spices of red beans and rice fame to the beloved olive salad on traditional muffaletta sandwiches.

3 large cloves garlic, crushed
1/3 cup coarsely chopped bell pepper
1/3 cup coarsely chopped celery
1/3 cup coarsely chopped onion
1/3 cup pecan pieces
1 (15-ounce) can dark red kidney
    beans, rinsed and drained
1/2 cup old-fashioned oats
1/2 cup vital wheat gluten
1 teaspoon lemon juice
3/4 teaspoon dried oregano

1/4 teaspoon dried basil
1/4 teaspoon sweet paprika
1/4 teaspoon dried thyme
1/4 teaspoon red pepper flakes
1/2 teaspoon sea salt
1/4 teaspoon freshly ground black pepper
Canola oil
4 whole grain buns, toasted
Creole Mayo (recipe follows)
Mixed Greens
Remoulade Relish (recipe follows)

1. In a food processor, combine the garlic, bell pepper, celery, onion, and pecans. Pulse to mince. Add the beans, oats, vital wheat gluten, lemon juice, oregano, basil, paprika, thyme, red pepper flakes, salt, and pepper. Process until well combined. Shape the mixture into 4 patties, about 3/4-inch thick, and transfer to a plate. Cover and refrigerate for 1 hour to firm up.

2. Heat a thin layer of canola oil in a large skillet over medium-high heat. Add the patties and cook for 5 minutes or until nicely browned. Use a spatula to turn the burgers and cook for 5 minutes on the other side.

3. *Assemble:* On the bottom bun halves, spread 1 tablespoon of the mayo and top with a small handful of mixed greens. Add the patties, a generous spoonful of Remoulade Relish, and another tablespoon of mayo. Arrange the remaining bun halves on top and serve immediately.

creole mayo

Yield: about 1/2 cup

1/2 cup vegan mayonnaise
1 tablespoon capers
1 clove roasted garlic (page 145)
2 teaspoons chili sauce
1 teaspoon Creole mustard
1/4 teaspoon fresh lemon juice

Dash Louisiana hot sauce
Dash vegan Worcestershire sauce or Bragg
    Liquid Aminos
Pinch chili powder
Pinch sea salt
Pinch white pepper

Combine all the ingredients in a small bowl. Set aside or cover and refrigerate until needed.

remoulade relish

Yield: about 1 cup

Look for pickled peppadews at the olive bar of well-stocked supermarkets. They are also available in jars in the pickle aisle.

1/3 cup oil-cured pitted black olives
1/3 cup brine-cured pitted green olives

1/3 cup pickled peppadew red peppers,
    cut into 1-inch pieces
3 scallions, minced

Place both kinds of olives and the peppers into a food processor and pulse a few times to coarsely chop. Transfer the mixture to a small bowl and fold in the scallions.

my big fat greek burgers

Yield: 4 servings

One of my most vivid food memories is sipping wine accompanied by fresh cucumber, tomatoes, and olives at a cliff-side vineyard on sun-drenched Santorini overlooking the sea. This burger is an ode to that experience and my love of all things Greek, not the least of which are the cuisine, the landscape, the art, and architecture.

3 large cloves garlic, crushed
1/3 cup coarsely chopped celery
1/3 cup coarsely chopped onion
1/4 cup coarsely chopped bell pepper
1 (15-ounce) can chickpeas, rinsed and
    drained
1/2 cup old-fashioned oats
1/2 cup vital wheat gluten
1/4 cup pine nuts
1 teaspoon fresh lemon juice

1 tablespoon dill weed
2 teaspoons dried oregano
1/2 teaspoon dried mint
1/2 teaspoon sea salt
1/4 teaspoon freshly ground black pepper
4 whole grain buns, toasted
Herbed Mayo (recipe follows) or Vegenaise
1 cup mixed salad greens
Tomato-Olive-Cucumber Relish (recipe fol-
    lows) or other relish, optional

1. In a food processor, combine the garlic, celery, onion, and bell pepper. Pulse to mince. Add the chickpeas, oats, vital wheat gluten, pine nuts, lemon juice, dill weed, oregano, mint, salt, and pepper. Process until well combined. Shape the mixture into 4 patties, about 3/4-inch thick, and transfer to a plate. Cover and refrigerate for 1 hour to firm up.

2. Heat a thin layer of canola oil in a large skillet over medium-high heat. Add the patties and cook 5 minutes or until nicely browned. Use a spatula to turn the burgers and cook 5 minutes on the other side.

3. On the bottom bun halves, spread 1 tablespoon of the mayo (if using), and top with small handful of mixed greens. Top with one of the patties, a generous spoonful of the relish, if using, and another tablespoon of the mayo. Arrange the remaining bun halves on top and serve immediately.

herbed mayo

Yield: about 1/2 cup

1/2 cup vegan mayonnaise
2 teaspoons fresh lemon juice
1 teaspoon red wine vinegar
2 teaspoons pomegranate molasses,
    optional
2 teaspoons minced fresh dill

2 teaspoons minced fresh mint
2 teaspoons minced fresh oregano
1 clove garlic, minced
Pinch natural sugar
Sea salt
White pepper

Combine all the ingredients in a small bowl. Set aside or cover and refrigerate until needed.

tomato-olive-cucumber relish

Yield: about 1 1/2 cups

2 Roma tomatoes, diced
1/2 cup chopped cucumber
1/4 cup chopped oil-cured black olives
1/4 cup chopped brine-cured green
    olives

Combine all the ingredients in a small bowl and mix gently. Use immediately, or cover and refrigerate until needed.

grilled eggplant and tofu sandwiches

Yield: 4 servings

The deep-flavored Roasted Red Onion Mayo is the perfect accompaniment to the delicious flavor of grilled summer eggplant. Brushing the eggplant slices with the marinade instead of truly marinating them prevents them from becoming too oily, yet allows them to absorb plenty of the paprika and aromatic turmeric. For best results, make the Roasted Red Onion Mayo in advance and refrigerate until needed.

4 1/2-inch thick slices eggplant
6 tablespoons olive oil
2 tablespoons balsamic or red wine vinegar
1 large clove garlic, minced
1 teaspoon sweet paprika
1 teaspoon turmeric

Sea salt and freshly ground black pepper
7 ounces extra-firm tofu, pressed, drained, patted dry, and cut into 1/4-inch thick slices
8 (1/2-inch thick) slices ciabatta bread, toasted or grilled
Roasted Red Onion Mayo (recipe follows)

1. Salt the eggplant slices and lay on a paper towel-lined baking sheet. Let sit for 30 minutes and then rinse, drain, and pat dry. In a small bowl, whisk together the oil, vinegar, garlic, paprika, turmeric, and salt and pepper to taste. Use a fork to lightly score both sides of the eggplant, brush both sides with the marinade, and stack two-deep on a plate.

2. Cover tightly with plastic wrap. Let the eggplant sit for 2 to 3 hours at room temperature, but no longer. Thirty minutes before you plan to grill the eggplant and tofu, brush the tofu slices with the marinade and place under the plastic wrap with the eggplant.

3. Preheat the oven to 250°F. Lightly oil a grill pan and place it over medium-high heat. Arrange the eggplant slices in the pan, press down lightly on them with a spatula and grill 3 to 5 minutes on each side or until nice grill marks develop and the eggplant is cooked through. Transfer the eggplant to a heatproof plate and keep warm in the oven. Grill the tofu using the same method, about 2 minutes per side.

4. Spread the bread slices with the mayo. Top 4 slices of bread with a slice of eggplant followed by a slice of tofu. Place the tops on each of the sandwiches, mayo side down, cut in half if desired, and serve immediately.

roasted red onion mayo

Yield: about 1 cup

1 tablespoon olive oil
1 small red onion, halved lengthwise,
    and cut into 1/4-inch slivers
Pinch sea salt
3 tablespoons vegan mayonnaise

1. Preheat the oven to 400°F. Combine the oil, onion, and salt in a baking pan and toss to coat. Roast for 15 to 20 minutes, stirring every 5 minutes, until onions are slightly shriveled and have developed some color. Transfer to a small bowl, and cool to room temperature.

2. In a small bowl, combine the onions with the mayo and stir to mix well.

mediterranean chickpea pita pockets

Yield: 4 servings

I created this sandwich for a picnic and kayak paddle in celebration of my husband's fortieth birthday. I brought it back more recently for an encore as part of a visit to the Virginia Museum of Fine Arts.

8 ounces extra-firm silken tofu
2 cups firmly packed fresh basil leaves
1/3 cup toasted slivered almonds
3 tablespoons fresh lemon juice
1 tablespoon olive oil
1/8 teaspoon garlic powder
1/8 teaspoon onion powder
1 tablespoon nutritional yeast, optional

Sea salt and freshly ground black pepper
1 (15.5-ounce) can chickpeas, rinsed and
    drained
4 whole wheat pita pockets, lightly
    warmed
1/2 cup Trish's Tangy Tapenade (page 24)
    or other tapenade

1. In a food processor, combine the tofu, basil, almonds, lemon juice, olive oil, garlic powder, onion powder, nutritional yeast, if using, and salt and pepper to taste. Process until almost smooth, scraping down the sides of the bowl as necessary.

2. In a medium bowl, combine 1/3 cup of the basil mixture with the chickpeas, adding more, if needed, to bind the chickpeas. Spoon the mixture into each pita pocket. Top each with 2 tablespoons tapenade and serve immediately.

tempeh salad sandwiches
with grapes and smoked almonds

Yield: 4 servings

Grapes add color, moisture, and natural sweetness to this hearty salad, while nuts add depth of flavor, crunch, and nutrition. In addition to being terrific in a whole grain sandwich, the filling is also great with crackers, celery sticks, or in a lettuce wrap. Some people prefer to steam their tempeh before using in recipes to mellow the flavor – this recipe allows for that option.

16 ounces tempeh
Sea salt
1 cup green seedless grapes, quartered
1/2 cup smoked almonds, coarsely
    chopped
1/2 cup chopped celery

2 tablespoons minced dill
6 tablespoons vegan mayonnaise
2 tablespoons maple syrup
1/4 teaspoon garlic powder
Freshly ground black pepper
8 slices whole grain bread

1. Preheat the broiler. Steam the tempeh for 10 minutes, if desired. Season both sides of the tempeh with salt and broil 2 to 3 minutes per side. Set aside until cool enough to handle.

2. In a medium bowl, combine the grapes, almonds, celery, dill, mayo, maple syrup, garlic powder, and salt and pepper to taste. Crumble the tempeh and add it to the bowl and combine gently with a fork to mix well. Taste and adjust the seasonings, if needed.

3. To serve, divide the mixture onto four slices of the bread, top each with another slice of bread, cut each sandwich in half and serve.

Variation

Make the recipe above with these substitutions: red grapes for green grapes; toasted walnuts for smoked almonds; orange bell pepper for celery; tarragon for dill.

waldorf-inspired smoky seitan sandwiches

Yield: 4 servings

This hearty sandwich filling gets its subtle wood-fired flavor from smoked almonds and smoked paprika. And the combination of crisp apples, celery, and carrots is a perfect accompaniment to a colorful fall day. Allowing the flavors to marry for a few hours before using in sandwiches enhances the flavor.

1 medium red apple, cored and cut into chunks
4 celery ribs, cut into chunks
1 small yellow onion, cut into chunks
2 carrots, cut into 1-inch pieces (about 3/4 cup)
1 1/2 cups smoked almonds
12 ounces seitan, cut into 1 1/2-inch pieces
3/4 cup lightly packed fresh parsley leaves

2 tablespoons fresh minced tarragon or 1 tablespoons dried
1 1/2 tablespoons nutritional yeast, optional
1 1/2 teaspoons vegetable broth powder
1 1/2 teaspoons smoked mild paprika
Pinch garlic powder
Sea salt and freshly ground black pepper
3/4 cup vegan mayonnaise
1 1/2 teaspoons fresh lemon juice
Bread of choice

1. Combine the apple, celery, onion, carrots, and almonds in a food processor. Process until coarsely chopped, scraping down the sides of the bowl as needed. Add the seitan, parsley, tarragon, nutritional yeast, if using, vegetable broth powder, smoked paprika, garlic powder, and salt and pepper to taste. Continue processing, using a pulsing action, scraping down the sides as necessary, until all of the ingredients are finely chopped.

2. Add the mayo and lemon juice and process just until the mixture comes together. Adjust the seasoning and pulse a few more times to combine.

3. To serve, spoon the seitan mixture onto bread or rolls of choice and serve immediately. If not using right away, cover and refrigerate until needed.

apricot-studded date-walnut spread sandwiches

Yield: 4 servings

Fresh and pretty, this sandwich would be lovely for afternoon tea, though it is a perfectly filling lunch when lighter fare is in order. Served here open-face on thin slices of pumpernickel, the luscious spread is also great on a toasted bagel for breakfast.

14 ounces firm tofu, drained and
    pressed
2 teaspoons lemon juice
1 1/2 teaspoons fresh grated ginger
2 teaspoons maple syrup
1 teaspoon vegan Worcestershire sauce
    or Bragg Liquid Aminos
3/4 teaspoon garlic powder
1/2 teaspoon ground cloves

1/4 teaspoon sea salt
Freshly ground black pepper
1 cup chopped pitted dates
1/2 cup chopped walnuts
1/2 cup chopped dried apricots
1 medium (8-ounce) cucumber, thinly sliced
Sea salt
8 slices Danish-style pumpernickel bread

In a food processor, combine the tofu, lemon juice, ginger, maple syrup, Worcestershire sauce, garlic powder, cloves, salt and pepper to taste, and process until smooth. Transfer to a medium bowl and stir in dates, walnuts, and apricots. Check for seasoning and adjust if necessary. Spread the mixture evenly onto the bread slices, top each with the cucumber slices, and sprinkle with pinch of sea salt. Serve immediately, two slices per serving.

Sandwiches with a Twist

In the mood for a sandwich with a twist? Why not peruse the Starters, Salads, and Brunch chapters for tasty dishes that could easily shape-shift into a sandwich.

broiled tofu sandwiches
with broccoli pesto

Yield: 4 servings

A crown of bright green broccoli pesto is a creamy foil for tender tofu and chewy ciabatta bread in this warm and wintry open-faced sandwich. **Note:** if your bread slices are small, allow two slices per serving, dividing the topping evenly among them.

5 ounces broccoli, coarsely chopped
14 ounces extra-firm tofu, drained, cut into 8 (1/2-inch) slices, and pressed
1 tablespoon olive oil, plus more for brushing tofu
Sea salt

1/4 cup toasted pumpkin seeds or pine nuts
1 tablespoon nutritional yeast
1 teaspoon lemon juice
2 tablespoons olive oil
4 (3/4-inch) slices of ciabatta or other rustic bread, lightly toasted

1. Preheat the broiler. Blanch or steam the broccoli until bright green and barely tender, about 3 minutes. Drain and set aside.

2. Arrange the tofu slices on an oiled baking sheet and brush with olive oil and sprinkle with salt on both sides. Broil the tofu for 6 to 7 minutes on each side. Watch closely to avoid burning. Set aside.

3. In a food processor, combine the reserved broccoli, pumpkin seeds, nutritional yeast, lemon juice, and 1/2 teaspoon of salt. Pulse to mix and create a textured paste. Drizzle in the 1 tablespoon olive oil and pulse a few more times to create a smoother paste. Check for seasoning and adjust as needed.

4. To assemble, arrange 2 pieces of tofu on each bread slice and top each with the pesto, dividing evenly. Broil the sandwiches for 1 minute to lightly heat the pesto. Serve hot with a knife and fork.

indian cauliflower wraps

Yield: 4 servings

This recipe was inspired by one of my favorite appetizers at Saffron Bistro, a local Indian restaurant. I often choose this delectable cauliflower (gobi) in its spicy red paste for a meal. In the original recipe, the cauliflower is battered and fried. Here, I roast it for a lighter version. The optional Ajwain seeds are commonly used in Indian cuisine. They are aromatic seeds reminiscent of thyme, but a little more bitter and pungent.

1 1/2 teaspoons toasted sesame oil
1 1/2 teaspoons olive oil
1 medium yellow onion, cut into 1/4-inch dice
Pinch sea salt
2 large cloves garlic, minced
1 (1-inch) piece fresh ginger, peeled and grated
1/2 teaspoon fresh minced green chile, optional
1 tablespoon water
1 tablespoon apple cider vinegar

1 tablespoon soy sauce
2 tablespoons catsup or chili sauce
1 teaspoon Ajwain seeds, optional
2 cups roasted cauliflower florets, cooled (see page 55)
2 scallions, sliced diagonally into 1/4-inch pieces
2 tablespoons coarsely chopped fresh cilantro
4 tablespoons vegan mayonnaise
2 cups tender salad greens
4 tortillas, pitas, or other vegan flatbread

1. Heat both oils in a large skillet over medium-high heat. Add the onion and cook, stirring, for 7 minutes, or until softened and slightly golden.

2. Reduce the heat to medium, season with salt to taste, and add the garlic, ginger, and chile, if using. Continue cooking for another minute or until the garlic is softened but not browned. Add the water, cider vinegar, soy sauce, catsup, and Ajwain seeds, if using. Stir and cook for 1 to 2 minutes or until the flavors are combined and the mixture is heated through.

3. Add the cauliflower and stir to coat well. Turn off the heat and stir in the scallions. Remove the pan from the heat and allow the mixture to cool for a few minutes. Stir in the cilantro and the mayo.

4. Arrange one quarter of the mixture and one quarter of the greens onto each flatbread. Roll up tightly and arrange on plates to serve.

blooming platter mayo

Yield: 1 1/2 cups

Buying prepared vegan mayonnaise can be expensive, so I make my own. Blooming Platter Mayo is light, flavorful, and can be used in any recipe calling for vegan mayonnaise.

12 ounces extra-firm silken tofu
1/2 teaspoon garlic powder
1/4 teaspoon onion powder
1 tablespoon fresh lemon juice
2 teaspoons apple cider vinegar
1/8 teaspoon sweet paprika

1/8 teaspoon turmeric
3/4 teaspoon sea salt
1/4 teaspoon fresh cracked black
    pepper or ground white pepper
1 teaspoon natural sugar
1 teaspoon nutritional yeast, optional

Combine all the ingredients in a food processor. Process until smooth, scraping down the sides as necessary. Adjust the seasoning as desired. Refrigerate until serving time.

sloppy tempeh sandwiches
with marinara mushrooms and spinach

Yield: 4 servings

Think of these sandwiches as very simple, but slightly dressed-up, Sloppy Joes. Crumbled tempeh makes the filling hearty, while mushrooms and marinara combined with a little vegan cream cheese create a velvety smooth sauce. Flecks of spinach provide a boost in nutrition and a beautiful color contrast to boot.

8 ounces tempeh
1 tablespoon olive oil
2 large cloves garlic, minced
3/4 cup marinara sauce
1/4 cup water
2 tablespoons vegan cream cheese

4 ounces white mushrooms, cut into
    1/4-inch slices
8 ounces baby spinach, coarsely chopped
Red pepper flakes (optional)
Sea salt
Freshly ground black pepper
4 crusty sandwich rolls, lightly toasted

Steam the tempeh for 15 minutes, if desired, to mellow the flavor. Heat the oil in a large skillet over medium-high heat. Crumble the tempeh into the skillet and cook, stirring continually, for 2 to 3 minutes or until golden brown. Add the garlic and cook, stirring, for 30 seconds. Stir in the marinara sauce, water, and cream cheese, and cook for 1 minute or until cream cheese melts and is completely combined. Add the mushrooms and cook, stirring frequently, for 4 to 5 minutes. Stir in the spinach, red pepper flakes, if using, and season with salt and pepper to taste. Cook, stirring until the spinach is wilted, about 30 seconds. To serve, spoon the mixture onto each roll, dividing evenly. Serve hot.

pear, walnut, and "blue cheese" sandwiches

Yield: 4 servings

I first enjoyed a vegetarian version of this open-faced sandwich years ago at a local French bistro. This version, made with warm pears, walnuts, and non-dairy "blue cheese," is just as memorable. For the bread in these sandwiches, I like to use something rustic like a ciabatta.

4 (3/4-inch thick) bread slices
4 teaspoons prepared brown mustard
1 large ripe pear, sliced lengthwise,
  cored, and cut into 1/4-inch slices

4 teaspoons light brown sugar
1/4 cup walnut pieces
1/4 cup "Blue Cheese" Sauce (recipe follows)

Preheat the broiler. Arrange the bread on a baking sheet. Spread each slice with 1 teaspoon mustard. Divide the pear slices among the bread slices in 1 or 2 layers and sprinkle with 1 teaspoon brown sugar. Broil for 1 minute to begin to melt the sugar. Remove the baking sheet from the oven, top each sandwich with one-quarter of walnut pieces, and then spoon one quarter of the cheese sauce over the top, trying not to let it run off of the bread. Broil for 2 minutes longer or until cheese sauce is hot and the walnuts are lightly toasted. Serve immmedaitely.

"blue cheese" sauce

Yield: 1 3/4 cups

In this version of blue cheese, beer is the secret ingredient that lends that elusive aged flavor. For best results, make this ahead of when you need it so the flavors have time to meld.

1/4 cup sesame tahini
1/4 cup roasted cashew pieces
1/4 cup plus 2 tablespoons beer or non-
  alcoholic beer
1/4 cup unsweetened soy milk
2 teaspoons white vinegar
1 tablespoon plus 1 teaspoon fresh
  lemon juice

1 teaspoon light-colored miso paste
1/4 teaspoon garlic powder
1/4 teaspoon onion powder
1/8 teaspoon sea salt
1/8 teaspoon white pepper
2 tablespoons minced fresh parsley
6 ounces extra-firm tofu, pressed, drained,
  and blotted dry

Combine all the ingredients except the parsley and tofu in a food processor. Process until smooth, scraping down the sides of the bowl as necessary. Transfer to a small bowl and stir in parsley. Break up the tofu and add to the bowl. Gently mash together, until the tofu chunks lose their uniform appearance. Use immediately or cover tightly and refrigerate until needed. Stir well before using.

Main Dishes

"A man seldom thinks with more earnestness of anything than he does of his dinner."

— Samuel Johnson

The Go-To Recipes...

A fresh, seasonal main dish can make an everyday meal extraordinary. In spring, I enjoy delicious calzones made with fresh asparagus and my signature white "cheese." I like Tempeh with Pecan-Tomato Sauce in summer and for Oktoberfest, I make tender-chewy vegan sausages accompanied by a tingly sweet apple sauerkraut and a sour cream horseradish sauce. When a winter chill is in the air, I find a simple fettuccine with caramelized onions and butternut squash comforting and satisfying. For easy menu planning, many of the recipes in this chapter offer suggestions for side dishes to celebrate the abundance of every season.

Main Dishes

pasta with broccoli, white beans, and sun-dried tomatoes

Yield: 4 servings

This dish is as pretty as it is satisfying with bright green broccoli and flecks of deep red sun-dried tomato playing off the creamy white of the pasta and beans.

4 ounces regular or whole wheat rotini
    or other bite-sized pasta
2 tablespoons olive oil
4 cloves garlic, minced
3 to 4 broccoli crowns, cut into small
    florets, (about 4 cups)
1 cup oil-packed sun-dried tomatoes,
    drained and cut into 1/4-inch strips

2 (15.5-ounce) cans white beans, rinsed
    and drained
4 tablespoons nutritional yeast
Sea salt and freshly ground black pepper
Red pepper flakes
1/4 cup toasted pine nuts, optional garnish

1. Cook the pasta in a 2-quart pot of boiling salted water until al dente, about 10 minutes. Drain and set aside, reserving about 1 cup of the pasta water.

2. Heat the oil in a large skillet over medium-high heat. Add the garlic, if using, and cook and stir until it sizzles. Add the broccoli and sauté for 3 to 5 minutes or until bright green and starting to crisp around the edges. Add the tomatoes, white beans, and 2 tablespoons of the pasta water. Stir in the cooked pasta, then sprinkle with the nutritional yeast. Season to taste with salt, pepper and red pepper flakes. Stir to combine, adding another 1 to 2 tablespoons of the pasta water if needed. Serve hot garnished with pine nuts, if using.

Variation

Instead of, or in addition to, the garlic cloves, add 1 tablespoon of vegan pesto when you combine the cooked ingredients.

---

caramelized onion and spinach quesadillas

Yield: 4 servings

You won't miss the cheese in these flavorful quesadillas made with a satisfying white bean mixture. Nutritionally balanced, these quesadillas can be enjoyed for lunch or dinner.

2 tablespoons vegan butter
4 (8-inch) whole wheat tortillas
1 cup White Bean "Cheese" (recipe follows)
2 cups fresh baby spinach leaves

1/2 cup caramelized onion (see note)
4 tablespoons vegan sour cream
4 tablespoons minced fresh cilantro

1. Preheat oven to 250°F. In a large skillet over medium-high heat, melt 1 tablespoon of the vegan butter.

2. Spread the tortillas with cheese leaving a 1/4-inch border. Top one half of each quesadilla with one-fourth of the spinach, followed by one-forth of the onion. Fold the other half of each tortilla over the spinach and onion and press down gently. Make two at a time by placing a pair of them in the skillet and frying on one side for a couple of minutes or until golden-brown and crispy, pressing down gently with a spatula to seal.

3. Carefully flip them and fry for another 2 minutes. Remove the quesadillas to a baking sheet and place in the oven to keep warm while preparing the remaining quesadillas.

4. When ready to serve, cut each quesadilla in half and arrange on plates. Top each with 1 tablespoon of vegan sour cream and sprinkle with 1 tablespoon of cilantro. Serve warm.

Note: To caramelize the onion, thinly slice a small yellow onion and sauté it in 1 tablespoon of olive oil in a large skillet over medium-high heat until golden-brown. Reduce the heat to medium and cook several minutes longer until the onions are very soft and the color has deepened.

white bean "cheese"

Yield: about 2 1/2 cups

Vegan block cheeses are available – and they are improving – but they are expensive, and I have yet to find one that I love. So, I've enjoyed experimenting with a variety of ingredients to create spreads that have a deep cheesy flavor and a good consistency. In addition to using on the quesadillas, this spread is delicious on sandwiches, toasts, and crackers.

1 cup cooked or canned cannellini
    beans, rinsed and drained
6 ounces firm silken tofu
1/4 cup nutritional yeast
2 tablespoons lightly salted roasted
    cashews
2 teaspoons fresh lemon juice

1 tablespoon olive oil
1 teaspoon garlic powder
1 teaspoon onion powder
2 tablespoons light miso paste
1/2 teaspoon turmeric, optional
1 tablespoon beer (or non-alcoholic beer)
1 tablespoon unsweetened soy milk

Combine all the ingredients in a food processor and process until the desired consistency is achieved, scraping down the sides of the bowl as necessary. Add up to 1 tablespoon additional beer and soy milk if you want a softer spread. Use immediately in the quesadillas or transfer to an airtight container and refrigerate until needed.

blooming vegetable calzones

Yield: 4 servings

Pizza dough is so easy and quick to make – most of the preparation time is hands-free rising time. This version is delicious as is, but consider it a springboard to develop your own tasty creations! If you like a gooey filling, feel free to substitute shredded vegan mozzarella for the white "cheese" in this recipe.

White "Cheese":
8 ounces firm tofu, drained and patted dry
2 teaspoons lemon zest
2 teaspoons nutritional yeast
1/4 teaspoon garlic powder
1/4 teaspoon onion powder
1/2 teaspoon dried basil
Pinch ground nutmeg
Sea salt and freshly ground black pepper

Filling:
2 tablespoons olive oil
1 small yellow onion, thinly sliced
Sea salt and freshly ground black pepper
6 ounces asparagus, chopped
1 red or yellow bell pepper, chopped
1 small zucchini, cut into 1/4-inch dice
4 cloves garlic, chopped
2 tablespoons Blooming Marinara Sauce
   (page 107) or other thick tomato
   sauce, plus more to serve
1/2 teaspoon dried oregano
Pizza Dough (page 99)

1. *White "Cheese":* Combine all of the ingredients in a medium bowl, and mash together, leaving some pieces of tofu in small chunks. Set aside. Preheat the oven to 450°F. Place a pizza stone or an inverted baking sheet in the oven and heat it for 30 minutes.

2. *Filling:* Heat 1 tablespoon of the oil in a large skillet over medium-high heat. Add the onion, season with salt and pepper and reduce the heat to medium. Cook, stirring, until onions are partially caramelized, about 10 minutes. Add water, 1 tablespoon at a time if needed, to prevent sticking. Add asparagus, bell pepper, and zucchini, and cook for 3 minutes or until softened but still brightly colored. Add the garlic and cook 2 minutes or until softened. Remove from the heat and stir in the 2 tablespoons tomato sauce and the oregano. Add the reserved cheese and stir to combine. Set aside.

3. *To Assemble:* Tear off two 10-inch sheets of aluminum foil, shiny side down. Spray each sheet lightly with non-stick spray. With hands lightly dusted with flour, divide the dough in half, shape each half into a ball, and place one in the center of each piece of foil.

4. Beginning in the center and working your way to the edges, use your fingertips and palms to gently press the dough into a circle about 8 1/2 inches in diameter. Spoon half of the filling mixture onto one half of the circle, leaving a generous 1/4-inch margin. Fold the remaining half of the dough over the filling and press the edges together to seal. Crimp with a fork and brush the surface of the dough with olive oil. Fold in the edges of the excess foil to make the calzone easier to lift and so that

both will fit on one stone or baking sheet. Repeat with the remaining dough ball and filling.

5. Using oven mitts, open the oven door and slide out the rack, then slide both calzones, foil and all, onto the hot stone or baking sheet. Bake for 11 minutes. Brush the tops again with the remaining oil, sprinkle with salt, and bake 4 minutes longer or until golden brown. Remove the calzones from the oven and transfer to a wire rack to cool for 10 minutes. Slice each calzone in half, top each half with about 2 tablespoons of marinara sauce and serve warm, one half per person. Serve a small bowl of marinara sauce on the side.

To Make Your Own Pizza Dough

Note: If you don't have self-rising flour, make your own by combining 1 cup all-purpose flour with 1 1/2 teaspoons baking powder and 1/4 teaspoon salt. Then proceed with the recipe.

3/4 cup plus 2 tablespoons self-rising flour (see note above)
3/4 cup plus 2 tablespoons whole wheat flour
1 teaspoon "quick rise" yeast
1 teaspoon natural sugar
1 teaspoon sea salt
3/4 cup plus 1 1/2 tablespoons tepid water
2 teaspoons extra virgin olive oil plus 1 teaspoon to oil the bowl

Place all of the dry ingredients in a large bowl, stir to combine, and make a well in the center. Add the water and 2 teaspoons olive oil to the well and stir the wet and dry ingredients together with a fork until fully incorporated.

Knead for 5 minutes with oiled hands or until the dough is smooth and elastic, but slightly sticky. I knead it right in the bowl. Do not over-knead. Lift out the dough and pour the remaining teaspoon of olive oil into the bottom of the bowl and spread with your fingers.

Return the dough to the bowl, rolling it around on both sides to coat with the oil. Cover the bowl loosely with a damp kitchen towel and allow the dough to rise until doubled in bulk, about 2 hours. While the dough rises, prepare other ingredients.

Yield: dough for 2 crusts

spicy baja tacos

Yield: 4 servings

Crunchy cabbage and jicama nestle in tortilla shells with crisp seitan strips and a gently spiced creamy sauce to create a fiesta of textures and tastes. Though the traditional filling is beer-battered, I prefer breading the seitan the way my parents fry fish: dipped in yellow mustard and then in flour or cornmeal. I use Panko bread crumbs for extra crispiness.

1/2 cup vegan sour cream
1/4 cup vegan mayonnaise
4 teaspoons capers, roughly chopped
1 teaspoon dry mustard
1/2 teaspoon ground cumin
1/8 teaspoon dried oregano, optional
Cayenne, to taste
1/3 cup finely chopped fresh dill weed
2 teaspoons lime juice
1/2 cup plus 1 tablespoon yellow pre-pared mustard

2 teaspoons kelp granules
1/2 cup plus 1 tablespoon Panko bread crumbs
12 ounces seitan (page 117), cut into 16 strips
1/2 cup finely shredded jicama
1/2 cup shredded cabbage
Optional garnish: 8 lime wedges and hot sauce
8 taco shells, storebought or homemade (page 101)

1. In a small bowl, combine the sour cream, mayo, capers, dry mustard, cumin, oreg-ano, if using, cayenne, dill weed, and lime juice. Stir until well mixed. Cover, and refrigerate until needed.

2. Combine the prepared mustard and kelp granules in a small bowl. Place the crumbs in another small bowl. Set a wire rack over a baking sheet. Coat each piece of seitan first with mustard and then with crumbs patting gently to coat. Transfer to the wire rack.

3. Reheat the oil in the skillet over medium-high heat. When the oil is hot, place half of the seitan fillets in the hot oil. Fry for 1 to 2 minutes or until golden brown. Turn and cook on the other side until golden. Drain on paper towel. Repeat with the remain-ing seitan.

4. Toss the jicama and cabbage together in a small bowl and set aside. Spoon a line of the Baja sauce into each taco shell and gently spread it up the sides. Fill the shell with about 2 tablespoons of jicama-cabbage mixture. Arrange two seitan fillets on top and spoon on a little more sauce.

5. Repeat with the remaining ingredients. Serve each taco with a wedge of lime and a sprinkling of hot sauce, if using.

To Make Homemade Taco Shells

If you want to make your own taco shells, they aren't difficult. When I have the extra time, I make them according to this recipe taught to me by my paternal grandmother.

  2 1/2 cups canola oil
  8 (6-inch) corn tortillas

Preheat the oven to 250°F. Heat the oil in a large skillet over medium-high heat. Fry the taco shells one at a time by holding one edge of the tortilla with your fingers or tongs while you lower the opposite edge into the pan until half of the tortilla is lying in the oil. Hold it in a kind of "U-shape," being careful not to burn yourself while the first side cooks for 2 to 3 minutes or until golden, but still flexible.

Release the side you have been holding, and flip the shell with tongs or a spatula and cook on the opposite side for an additional 2 to 3 minutes. Shells should be crispy-chewy, but flexible. Drain on a paper towel-lined plate and repeat with remaining tortillas. Keep warm in the oven.

Yield: Makes 8 shells

indian eggplant paneer

Yield: 4 to 6 servings

Before there were Indian restaurants in Virginia Beach, I had to satisfy my cravings by learning to make my favorite creations at home. In this dish, enjoy a non-dairy version of paneer, a fresh cheese commonly featured in authentic Indian cuisine. Serve with freshly cooked basmati rice.

1 tablespoon canola oil
1 medium onion, cut into 1/4-inch dice
2 large cloves garlic, minced
1 (15-ounce) can fire-roasted tomatoes, undrained
3/4 cup water
1 medium eggplant, cut into 3/4-inch dice
1 tablespoon garam marsala
2 teaspoons ground coriander
1 teaspoon ground cardamom

1 teaspoon ground cumin
1 teaspoon turmeric
1 teaspoon sugar
1/4 cup coarsely chopped fresh cilantro
2 tablespoons soy creamer
1 teaspoon minced jalapeño
7 ounces extra-firm tofu, pressed, drained, blotted dry, and cut into 1-inch cubes
Optional Garnish: fresh cilantro leaves and 2 tablespoons roasted cashews

1. Heat the oil in a large skillet over medium-high heat. Add the onion and sauté for 10 minutes or until golden brown. Add 2 to 3 tablespoons of water during the cooking time to help prevent the onions from scorching. Add the garlic and continue to sauté for 2 minutes. Add the tomatoes, water, eggplant, garam marsala, coriander, cardamom, cumin, turmeric, and sugar, and simmer, stirring occasionally, for 20 minutes.

2. Stir in the cilantro and soy creamer and simmer, stirring occasionally, for 5 minutes. Add the jalapeño, stirring to incorporate well. Fold in the tofu and cook until heated through, about 5 minutes. Transfer to a shallow serving bowl. Garnish with cilantro and cashews, if using. Serve hot.

angel hair pasta
with chard and bell peppers

Yield: 4 servings

Fresh ingredients and pantry staples create a beautiful and nutritious dinner on the fly. This dish is equally delicious – if not more so – the next day.

8 ounces whole wheat angel hair pasta
1 tablespoon olive oil
2 large cloves garlic, minced
1 yellow or orange bell pepper, cut into
    1-inch pieces
4 ounces stemmed chard, finely chopped
1 cup grape tomatoes, halved

1/4 cup plus 2 tablespoons nutritional yeast
Sea salt and freshly ground black pepper
1/2 cup pasta water
2 tablespoons fresh basil chiffonade
2 teaspoons lemon zest
Optional garnish: 2 tablespoons toasted
    pine nuts

1. Add the pasta to a large pot of boiling salted water. Reduce the heat to a simmer, cook until tender, 6 to 7 minutes. Drain, reserving 1/2 cup of the pasta water. Set aside.

2. Heat the oil in a large skillet over medium heat. Add the garlic and sauté for 30 seconds or until golden. Add the bell pepper and sauté for 2 minutes or until it becomes slightly tender. Add the chard and sauté for 2 minutes, or until the chard is tender but retains its bright color.

3. Add the tomatoes and heat through. Add the nutritional yeast and the reserved pasta water. Stir and heat the sauce until it comes together. Check for seasoning and add salt and pepper to taste. Stir in the reserved pasta, basil, and lemon zest. Serve immediately garnished with pine nuts, if using.

southwestern tempeh and corn pie

Yield: 6 to 8 servings

This crowd-pleasing dish is rustic and hearty from the cornmeal crust to the savory filling. I like it best served with sautéed greens on the side to make a complete meal.

Crust:
3/4 cup unbleached all-purpose or
    whole wheat flour
3/4 cup plain or self-rising cornmeal
1/4 teaspoon chili powder or to taste
1 teaspoon salt
1/2 cup canola oil
2 tablespoons unsweetened soy milk

Filling:
1 tablespoon olive oil
1 medium yellow onion, chopped
4 cloves garlic, minced
12 ounces tempeh, crumbled (about 1
    1/2 cups)

1 1/2 cups fresh corn kernels
1 pound extra-firm silken tofu, drained
1/2 cup unsweetened soy milk
1/2 teaspoon ground cumin
1/2 teaspoon ground coriander
2 tablespoons nutritional yeast
3 tablespoons minced fresh parsley, optional
Sea salt and freshly ground black pepper
1/2 red or orange bell pepper, cut into
    strips
1/2 cup vegan sour cream
Zest and juice of 1/2 lime
Chipotle chili powder, for garnish

1. **Crust:** Preheat the oven to 400°F. Combine the dry ingredients in a 9-inch deep dish pie plate and make a well in the center. Pour the oil and soy milk into the well and combine the wet and dry ingredients with a fork until all of the liquid is absorbed. Press the crust firmly into the bottom and sides of the pie plate. Bake the crust for 10 minutes, then remove from the oven, but leave the oven on.

2. **Filling:** Heat the oil in a large skillet over medium-high heat. Add the onion and garlic and sauté until golden. Stir in the tempeh and cook until lightly browned, about 5 minutes. Stir in the corn and cook 1 minute longer. Set aside.

3. In a food processor combine tofu, soy milk, cumin, coriander, nutritional yeast, and parsley, if using. Season with salt and pepper to taste. Process until smooth, scraping down sides as needed. In a large bowl combine tofu mixture with the tempeh. Transfer into the reserved crust and smooth the top. Bake 35 to 40 minutes, or until set.

4. After 15 to 20 minutes, remove the pie from the oven and arrange bell pepper strips in a pinwheel on top, gently pressing to partially submerge. Return to the oven to finish baking.

5. In a small bowl, combine the sour cream, lime juice and zest, and salt and pepper to taste. Mix well. Let the pie stand for at least 5 minutes before cutting. When ready to serve, spoon the sour cream onto the pie and sprinkle with the chili powder.

tofu with tomato-caper wine sauce

Yield 4 servings

This luscious wine sauce is a zesty complement to sautéed tofu served atop freshly cooked brown rice. It's also great spooned over sautéed tempeh or seitan. Roasted zucchini or asparagus makes a good accompaniment.

2 tablespoons olive oil, divided
1 pound extra-firm tofu, drained, cut into 1/2-inch slices, and pressed
Sea salt and freshly ground black pepper
4 large cloves garlic, minced
2 cups Reisling or other white wine
2 teaspoons vegan Worcestershire sauce or Bragg Liquid Aminos
2 teaspoons brown rice syrup

2 tablespoons vegan butter
4 Roma tomatoes, cut into 1/4-inch dice
2 tablespoon capers
1/4 cup plus 2 tablespoons fresh minced parsley
2 teaspoons arrowroot powder dissolved in 1 tablespoon cold water
2 teaspoons fresh lemon juice

1. Preheat the oven to 250°F. Heat 1 tablespoon of oil in a large skillet over medium-high heat. Add the tofu, in batches if necessary, and sauté until golden brown on both sides. Season with salt and pepper to taste. Transfer to a heatproof platter and keep warm in the oven.

2. Heat the remaining 1 tablespoon of oil in the same skillet. Add the garlic and sauté for 30 seconds. Add the wine and cook until it is reduced by half. Stir in the Worcestershire sauce, brown rice syrup, vegan butter, tomatoes, capers, and parsley. Season with salt to taste and cook for 2 minutes or until the tomatoes are heated through.

3. Add the arrowroot-water mixture to the skillet and cook, stirring, for 1 minute to thicken. Avoid cooking longer, as the arrowroot will lose its thickening power. Remove the pan from the heat and stir in the lemon juice. To serve, spoon the sauce over the warm tofu and serve immediately.

zucchini-stuffed shells
with blooming marinara sauce

Yield: 4 servings

My mom used to make a wonderful zucchini, Swiss cheese, and torn bread filling that I adored as a vegetarian. As a vegan, I combine the grated zucchini with caraway seeds and an ultra-creamy sauce to capture something of the same taste and texture. I think you'll love these tender shells bursting with filling and nestled into a vibrant marinara sauce. To save time, a store-bought marinara sauce may be used instead of the one in this recipe.

12 jumbo dried pasta shells
Sea salt
1 tablespoon olive oil
4 shallots, halved and sliced thinly
3 cloves garlic
4 small (6-inch) zucchini
1 teaspoon caraway seeds

1 tablespoon balsamic vinegar or balsamic reduction
2 teaspoons lemon zest
Cauli-fredo Sauce (recipe follows)
Blooming Marinara Sauce, gently heated (recipe follows)
Fresh parsley sprigs, for garnish

1. Lightly oil a 9x13-inch baking dish and set aside. Cook the pasta shells in a 4-quart saucepan of boiling salted water until al dente, 12 to 15 minutes. Drain, rinse with cold water, and drain again.

2. Heat the oil in a large skillet over medium-high heat. Add the shallots and garlic and sauté until softened, 1 to 2 minutes. Add the zucchini, caraway seeds, and salt to taste, and cook, stirring, until moisture is released and most of it has evaporated, 5 to 7 minutes. Add the vinegar and cook another minute.

3. Remove the skillet from the heat and stir in lemon zest. Add about 1/4 cup of the Cauli-fredo Sauce to the zucchini mixture and stir to mix well. Keep the remaining sauce warm. Stuff each shell with about 2 tablespoons of the filling. Preheat the oven to 350°F.

4. Spoon a layer of heated marinara sauce into the bottom of the prepared baking dish and nestle the stuffed shells into the sauce. Cover with foil and bake for 20 minutes or until warm throughout. Serve immediately topped with the remaining Cauli-fredo Sauce, followed by a drizzle of the remaining marinara, if desired, and garnish with parsley.

cauli-fredo sauce

Yield: about 2 1/2 cups

1 tablespoon plus 1 teaspoon olive oil
1 small onion, chopped
1 cup cooked cauliflower florets
6 ounces firm silken tofu
2 tablespoons roasted and lightly salted
    cashew pieces
1 teaspoon fresh lemon juice

1 teaspoon apple cider vinegar
1 teaspoon garlic powder
1 teaspoon onion powder
1/4 teaspoon celery seed
Pinch nutmeg
1/2 teaspoon sea salt
1/8 teaspoon white pepper

Heat the 1 teaspoon olive oil in a small skillet over medium-high heat. Add the onion and cook until softened, about 5 minutes. Transfer the onion to a food processor. Add the remaining ingredients and process until the mixture is smooth, scraping down the sides of bowl as needed. Transfer the mixture to a 1 quart saucepan over medium heat and warm through, stirring frequently. The sauce can be used immediately or stored for up to 3 days in an airtight container in the refrigerator.

blooming marinara sauce

Yield: about 4 cups

1 medium onion, cut into chunks
4 cloves garlic
1 cup baby carrots
1 small red bell pepper, stemmed and
    seeded
1 tablespoon olive oil
1 (14.5-ounce) can fire-roasted crushed
    tomatoes, undrained

3/4 cup water
2 tablespoons maple syrup
1 teaspoon dried basil
1 teaspoon dried oregano
Pinch onion powder
Salt and freshly ground black pepper

1. Combine the onion, garlic, carrots, and bell pepper in a food processor and process until smooth, scraping down the sides of bowl as needed.

2. Heat the oil in a large skillet over medium-high heat. Add the onion mixture and sauté for about 10 minutes or until the vegetables are softened, and some of the moisture has evaporated. Reduce the heat if necessary to prevent sticking. Add the tomatoes, water, maple syrup, basil, oregano, onion powder, and salt and pepper to taste. Simmer 15 minutes, or until flavors have melded and the sauce is hot.

tempeh with pecan-tomato sauce

Yield: 4 servings

Absolutely packed with protein, this pretty dish feels special enough to serve to guests. I prefer wild rice tempeh for this recipe, but any variety may be used. For a more mellow tempeh flavor, steam or simmer the tempeh for 15 minutes before using.

3 tablespoons olive oil
1/3 cup whole-wheat flour
Pinch garlic powder
Pinch onion powder
Sea salt and freshly ground black pepper
2 (8-ounce) packages tempeh, each cut
   crosswise into 4 equal pieces

1 cup vegetable stock
2 tablespoons dry sherry wine
1/3 cup fresh minced parsley
16 grape tomatoes, halved lengthwise
1/4 cup pecan halves or pieces

1. Preheat the oven to 250°F, then turn it off, but leave the door closed.

2. Heat the oil in a large skillet over medium-high heat. In a small bowl, combine the flour with a generous pinch each of garlic powder, onion powder, salt, and pepper. Dredge the tempeh in the flour mixture and arrange in the hot skillet. Cook until golden brown on both sides, about 5 minutes per side, adding more oil if needed. Reserve the dredging flour. Transfer the tempeh to a platter and keep warm in the oven.

3. Reheat the same skillet over medium-high heat. Add 2 teaspoons of the remaining dredging flour and stir to pick up the remaining oil from the surface of the skillet. Add the stock and simmer, stirring continuously, until the sauce thickens slightly. Stir in the sherry and parsley followed by the tomatoes. Cook and stir until they are heated through, about 1 minute. Stir in the pecans and cook 1 minute longer. To serve, spoon the sauce over the warm tempeh and serve immediately.

Blooming Vegetable Calzones, 98

Mango-Coconut Cream Sorbet, 151

Sassy Springtime Rolls, 19

Fresh Strawberry Pancakes, 177

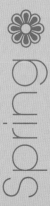

Chocolate Carrot Cake, 149

Spinach Tortilla Soup, 61

Grilled Radishes and Spring Greens with Maple-Curry Vinaigrette, 40

Macadamia Shortbread Tart
with Lemon Mousse and Fresh Berries, 156

Black Bean and Roasted Corn Salad, 44

Grilled Eggplant with Tahini-Paprika Sauce, 130

Zucchini-Stuffed Shells
with Blooming Marinara Sauce, 106

Bourbon-Broiled Peaches, 157

Blueberry and Lemon Verbena Pancakes, 185

Summer

Angel Hair Pasta with Chard and Bell Peppers, 103

Baked Apples Baklava with Cider Sauce, 162

Moroccan Eggplant
and Red Bell Pepper Salad, 53

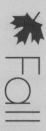
Fall

Beet Muhummara, 27

Sweet Potato Layer Cake
with Butterscotch-Bourbon Cream, 166

Fall

Farmstand Fruit Muffins, 194

Sweet Potatoes Caribbean, 138

Butternut Squash Bisque with Cranberry Gremolata, 66

Curried Couscous, 140

Indian Cauliflower with Black Mustard Seeds, 140

Ginger Streusel Pear Pie, 170

Winter ❄

Chocolate-Orange Mousse, 169

Sage-Scented Fettuccine
with Butternut Squash, 118

Kung Pao Broccoli and Tofu, 119

seitan and mushrooms
with broccoli in creamy tarragon sauce

Yield: 4 servings

This recipe makes a warm, comforting meal that tastes decadent, but is easy to put together on a chilly fall night. Although this dish can be served over rice or pasta, I highly recommend serving it with the Lazy Paprika Palmiers (below). A side salad also goes well with this meal.

1 tablespoon olive oil
3 to 4 cloves garlic, thinly sliced
1 cup sliced white mushrooms
1 small yellow bell pepper, sliced length-
    wise into 1/4-inch strips
2 cups small broccoli florets
3 tablespoons nutritional yeast

3 tablespoons all-purpose flour
1/4 cup dry white wine
1 cup plain unsweetened soy creamer
1 to 2 tablespoons dried tarragon
8 ounces seitan (page 117) cut into strips
Sea salt and freshly ground black pepper

1. Heat the oil in a large skillet over medium heat. Add the garlic and cook, stirring constantly, for 30 seconds until it is lightly colored. Add the mushrooms, and sauté for about 5 minutes until the moisture is released and has evaporated and the mushrooms begin to brown. Add the bell pepper strips and broccoli and sauté for 2 minutes. Sprinkle the mixture with nutritional yeast and flour, and stir to distribute evenly. Add the white wine and stir to dissolve the yeast and flour.

2. Immediately add the soy creamer and tarragon and cook, stirring constantly, another 3 to 4 minutes until the mixture thickens and the flour loses its raw taste. The broccoli should still be bright green but tender. Stir in the seitan and heat through. Season with salt and pepper to taste. Serve hot.

Lazy Paprika Palmiers

This short-cut version of palmiers is a quick and easy alternative to hot baked rolls. All you need is 1 sheet of Pepperidge Farm Puff Pastry, thawed, and some paprika. Preheat the oven to 400°F. Keeping the pastry double-folded as it comes out of the package, cut the dough crosswise into 8 equal pieces, about 1-inch wide. Arrange on an ungreased baking sheet, spaced as far apart as possible. Sprinkle lightly with paprika. Bake for 15 minutes or until puffed and golden. Remove to a wire rack to cool. Serve hot.

white bean sausages
with red apple sauerkraut

Yield: 4 servings

A vegan Oktoberfest may sound like an oxymoron. But, thanks to a simple white bean sausage recipe (for those who love to cook) or prepared vegan brats (for those who don't) – everyone can take part in the merrymaking. A zesty apple sauerkraut and a creamy horseradish sauce are paired with the sausages. The Braised Cabbage, Apples, and Potatoes (page 134) are also an ideal accompaniment.

1 1/2 cups white beans, rinsed and drained
2 cloves garlic, minced
1 cup vegetable broth
1 tablespoon olive oil
1 teaspoon vegan Worcestershire sauce or Bragg Liquid Aminos
1/2 teaspoon Liquid Smoke
1 1/2 cups vital wheat gluten
1/2 teaspoon coarse sea salt

1/2 teaspoon dried marjoram
1/2 teaspoon coriander seeds
1/2 teaspoon caraway seeds
1/4 teaspoon mace
Pinch white pepper
Sour Cream-Horseradish Sauce (recipe follows)
Red Apple Sauerkraut (recipe follows) or regular sauerkraut

1. Tear off 4 sheets of foil about 6 inches wide. Place a steamer basket in a 4-quart saucepan and fill with water just to the bottom of the steamer. Cover the pan and bring the water to a boil over medium-high heat. Reduce the heat to a simmer.

2. In a medium bowl, mash the beans and garlic until creamy. A few small pieces of beans may remain. Stir in the vegetable broth, olive oil, Worcestershire sauce, and Liquid Smoke. Set aside. In another medium bowl, whisk together vital wheat gluten, salt, marjoram, coriander, caraway, mace, and white pepper.

3. Pour the bean mixture into a well in the center of the dry ingredients and, using a fork, stir the dry ingredients around the edge of the bowl into the wet center until all of the ingredients are completely combined.

4. Divide the dough into four equal parts. Place each part on a sheet of foil and shape into 5 to 6-inch long logs about 1 1/2 inches in diameter. Lay each log along one long edge of the foil and roll snugly, bending up the foil at the ends. Place the logs into the steamer and steam for 40 minutes, adding more hot water to the saucepan if necessary to prevent it from evaporating completely.

5. Remove the sausages from the steamer and unroll them when cool enough to handle. Be careful that you don't burn yourself with escaping steam. Serve the sausages with the horseradish sauce and sauerkraut.

sour cream-horseradish sauce

Yield: 1 cup

You may make more or less of this tasty sauce; just use equal parts vegan sour cream and prepared horseradish.

1/2 cup vegan sour cream
1/2 cup prepared horseradish (not cream-style, as it is not vegan)

Combine the sour cream and horseradish in a small bowl and stir until well blended. Use immediately or cover and refrigerate until needed.

red apple sauerkraut

Yield: about 2 1/2 cups

1 tablespoon olive oil
3/4 cup apple cider vinegar
1/4 cup red table wine
2 tablespoons brown sugar
1 teaspoon whole yellow mustard seeds
2 large red delicious apples, skin-on, quartered, cored and grated
Sea salt and freshly ground black pepper

In a 2-quart saucepan, combine the oil, vinegar, wine, and sugar over medium-high heat, and cook until the sugar has dissolved. Add the mustard seeds, apples, and salt and pepper to taste. Simmer for 15 minutes, then set aside to cool. Serve with a slotted spoon or a fork. Store in the refrigerator in an airtight container.

pumpkin-stuffed shells with sage butter

Yield: 6 servings

I always find pumpkin ravioli with sage butter and similar dishes utterly seductive on restaurant menus but, alas, they are never vegan. This streamlined version is perfect for weeknight meals at home. The pumpkin filling bakes into a luscious custard in pasta shells. A luxurious drizzle of vegan sage butter over the top is exactly the right counterpoint.

Pumpkin Filling:
1 tablespoon olive oil
1 small onion, sliced
2 large cloves garlic, sliced
1 (15-ounce) can pureed pumpkin
1 (12-ounce) box firm silken tofu
1 tablespoon all-purpose flour
Sea salt and freshly ground black pepper
1 teaspoon onion powder
1/2 teaspoon garlic powder
1 tablespoon nutritional yeast
Generous pinch of nutmeg

1 tablespoon light miso paste
3 cups marinara sauce (page 107) or
    storebought

Sage Butter:
1/4 cup vegan butter
3 tablespoons fresh minced sage or 1
    tablespoon dried

To Assemble:
18 jumbo pasta shells
1 tablespoon toasted pine nuts, optional
    garnish

1. **Filling:** Heat the oil in a large skillet over medium-high heat. Add onion and garlic, and sauté until softened and onion begins to turn golden, about 5 minutes. Transfer the onion mixture to a food processor along with remaining ingredients. Add 2 tablespoons of the marinara sauce, and process until smooth, scraping down the sides of the bowl as necessary. Set aside.

2. **Sage Butter:** Heat the butter in a small skillet over medium-high until melted and starting to brown. Add sage, stir well, and remove from heat. Set aside.

3. **To Assemble:** Oil the bottom and sides of a shallow 9 x 13-inch baking dish. Cook the shells in a pot of boiling salted water until al dente, 12 to 15 minutes. Drain, rinse with cold water, and drain again. Preheat the oven to 350°F. Pour the marinara sauce into bottom of baking dish. Fill each shell with the pumpkin filling and nestle into the sauce. Bake uncovered for 25 minutes. Drizzle the sage butter over the pumpkin filling and bake the shells, uncovered, 5 minutes longer. Garnish with pine nuts, if using. Serve hot.

Variation

To deepen the earthy flavor, add 1/2 cup of sautéed mushrooms spooned between the shells, just before serving time.

roasted butternut pizza
with caramelized onions

Yield: 4 servings (2 small pizzas)

In the fall, it seems I want to use roasted or caramelized squash and onions in every dish I make. This pizza is one reason why. Green flecks of pine-scented fresh rosemary leaves are beautiful against the golden crust and topping of this earthy-sweet and mellow pie. It gets a little kick from optional red pepper flakes and extra creaminess from homemade vegan white cheese.

Topping:
1 small butternut squash, halved lengthwise
1 tablespoon olive oil
1 small red onion, cut into 1/4-inch slices
Sea salt

Creamy "White Cheese":
3/4 cup roasted cashews
1/4 cup plus 2 tablespoons beer (or non-alcoholic beer)
1/4 cup unsweetened soy milk

1 teaspoon light miso paste
1/4 teaspoon prepared mustard
1 tablespoon nutritional yeast
1 teaspoon fresh lemon juice
Pinch garlic powder
Pinch white pepper
Pinch sea salt
6 ounces firm silken tofu
Rosemary Olive Oil for brushing (page 114), optional
Pizza Dough (page 99) or prepared dough

1. **Topping:** Remove the seeds and pulp from the squash, peel, and cut each half crosswise into 1/4-inch slices.

2. Preheat the oven to 400°F. In a large roasting pan, combine the squash with the oil and the onion. Toss to coat the vegetables with the oil. Add salt to taste and toss again. Roast for 30 minutes, stirring after every 10 minutes. Remove from oven and allow the vegetables to cool. While they are roasting, make the cheese.

3. **Creamy "White Cheese":** In a food processor, combine all of the ingredients except the tofu. Process until smooth, scraping down the sides of the bowl as necessary. Transfer to a small bowl and mash the tofu into the mixture. Stir well to distribute. Cover and refrigerate until needed.

4. **Shape Dough:** After the dough has risen, preheat the oven to 450°F. Place two pizza stones or inverted baking sheets inside and heat them for 30 minutes. Divide the dough in half, shape each half into a ball, dust lightly with flour, and place each in the center of a lightly oiled piece of foil about 10 inches square, shiny side down. Starting with one ball, begin in the center and working your way to the edges, use your fingertips to gently press and stretch the dough into an 8 1/2-inch circle with a slightly raised rim. Repeat with the remaining dough and foil.

5. Spread about 1/3 cup of the cheese sauce onto each crust to make a thin layer, leaving a 1/2-inch margin. Top each pizza evenly with half of the roasted squash and onions. Arrange the squash in a kind of pinwheel design, if desired. Dot each pizza with a few more cheese chunks. Brush the rim of the crust with the Rosemary Olive Oil, if using, and dot some of the oil on the squash and onions. Using oven mitts, open the oven door and slide out the rack(s). Carefully slide each pizza, foil and all, onto a pizza stone or baking sheet. Slide the racks back into place and bake for about 11 minutes.

6. When the crusts are just golden, remove the pizzas from the oven. Brush the rims with a little more oil if desired and sprinkle the pizzas with some of the rosemary leaves that have been marinating in the oil. Allow the pies to cool for a couple of minutes and then slide them off of the foil and onto serving platters. Serve warm.

Rosemary Olive Oil

1/4 cup olive oil
1 tablespoon fresh rosemary leaves

Pour the olive oil into a small cup or bowl. Crush the rosemary leaves with your fingers and add them to the olive oil. Set the mixture aside until ready to use. The longer it steeps, the more intense the rosemary flavor will be.

"white cheese" pizza with kale and sun-dried tomatoes

Yield: 4 servings (2 small pizzas)

This beautiful and healthy pizza is bursting with fresh flavors. I enjoy it every winter when kale is in abundance.

1 bunch kale (6 ounces), thick stems removed
1 tablespoon olive oil
Pizza Dough (page 99) or prepared pizza dough

2/3 cup Creamy "White Cheese" (page 113)
6 to 8 sundried tomatoes in oil, drained and halved
Rosemary Olive Oil (page 114), optional

1. Working in batches, finely chop the kale in a food processor and set aside. Heat the olive oil in a large skillet over medium-high heat. Add the kale, and sauté until tender, bright green, and begins to develop tiny crispy bits, 3 to 4 minutes. Remove from the heat and set aside.

2. *Shape dough:* After the dough has risen, preheat the oven to 450°F and place pizza stones or an inverted baking sheet inside. Preheat them for 30 minutes. Divide the dough in half, shape each half into a ball, dust lightly with flour, and place in the center of a lightly oiled piece of foil about 10 inches square, shiny side down. Starting with one ball, begin in the center and, working your way to the edges, use your fingertips to gently press and stretch dough into an 8 1/2-inch circle with a slightly raised rim. Repeat with the other half of dough on the other piece of foil.

3. *Assemble and bake pizzas:* Spread about 1/3 cup of the cheese sauce on each crust to make a thin layer, leaving a 1/2-inch margin. Top each pizza evenly with half of the sautéed kale and half of the remaining cheese sauce. Brush the rim of the crust with olive oil or rosemary olive oil, if using.

4. Using oven mitts, open the oven door and slide out the rack(s). Carefully slide each pizza, foil and all, onto its pizza stone or inverted baking sheet. Slide the rack(s) back into place and bake the pizzas for about 10 minutes or until the crusts are golden. Sprinkle the sun-dried tomatoes over the top and return to the oven for 1 minute longer. Remove the pizzas from the oven. Brush with a little more oil if desired. Allow the pizzas to cool for 2 to 3 minutes, then slide them off of the foil onto serving platters. Cut into quarters and serve warm.

seitan and kale in coconut sauce

Yield: 4 servings

I return to this delicious dinner again and again. I love the combination of flavorful seitan and bright green kale. Served over golden Curried Couscous (page 140), this fragrant and lovely dish is truly more than the sum of its parts.

8 cups water
Sea salt
10 ounces kale, stemmed and coarsely chopped
1 tablespoon olive oil
1 medium yellow onion, halved and slivered
8 ounces seitan (see page 117), cut into strips

1 (15-ounce) can unsweetened coconut milk
2 tablespoons fresh lime juice
2 tablespoons natural sugar
1/4 teaspoon garlic powder
Freshly ground black pepper
Curried Couscous (page 140), optional

1. In a 4-quart saucepan, bring the water and a generous pinch of salt to boil over medium-high heat. Add the kale, stir well, and simmer for 8 minutes or until softened, but still green. Drain and set aside.

2. Heat the oil in a large skillet over medium-high heat. Add the onion and sauté until it softens, 3 minutes. Add the reserved kale and sauté 3 minutes longer. Add the seitan, coconut milk, lime juice, sugar, garlic powder, and salt and pepper to taste. Cook, stirring frequently, until the ingredients are heated through but the kale is still bright green, about 5 minutes. Taste and adjust the seasonings if needed. Serve hot over couscous, if using.

Blooming Platter Seitan

Yield: about 1 1/2 pounds seitan

Lightly seasoned with herbs, this is my "go-to" seitan recipe. It can be used in any of the recipes in this book that call for seitan. I like to keep a batch in my freezer so I always have some on hand.

    4 cups plus 1 cup water, divided
    2 tablespoons vegetable broth powder
    2 garlic cloves, crushed
    2 bay leaves
    1 tablespoon vegan Worcestershire sauce or Bragg Liquid Aminos
    1 tablespoon dried parsley
    1 teaspoon celery salt
    1 cup vital wheat gluten
    1 teaspoon nutritional yeast
    1/4 teaspoon garlic powder
    1/4 teaspoon rubbed sage
    1/8 teaspoon ground thyme
    1/4 teaspoon sea salt

In a 4-quart pot over medium-high heat, combine the 4 cups water, vegetable broth powder, garlic, bay leaves, Worcestershire sauce, parsley, and celery salt. Loosely cover and bring to a gentle boil; then reduce heat to a simmer.

In a medium bowl, combine the vital wheat gluten with the nutritional yeast, garlic powder, sage, thyme, and salt. Slowly add the remaining 1 cup of water, stirring until well combined. Knead right in the bowl for 3 minutes.

On a work surface, shape the seitan into a 3 x 5-inch loaf. Divide the loaf into eight pieces for cutlets, or cut it into strips, using a serrated knife. Add the seitan to the simmering broth, gently stretching each piece as you add it. Simmer for approximately 50 minutes, stirring every 15 minutes, or until much of the liquid has evaporated. Do not allow all of the liquid to evaporate, or the seitan will stick to the bottom of the pan and scorch.

At this point, the seitan may be used in recipes. If not using right away, set aside to cool, then cover tightly and refrigerate or freeze until needed.

sage-scented fettuccine
with butternut squash

Yield: 4 servings

This light recipe places golden squash center stage and uses just enough pasta to hold the dish together. I recommend using whole wheat pasta, as its nuttiness contributes significantly to the distinctive flavor of this dish.

2 tablespoons olive oil, divided
1 pound butternut squash, peeled,
     seeded, quartered lengthwise, and
     cut into 1/4-inch thick slices
Sea salt
1 cup vegetable stock
1 yellow onion, halved and cut into 1/4-
     inch slices
1/4 cup white wine

1 tablespoon maple syrup
1 tablespoon balsamic vinegar
2 teaspoons rubbed sage
4 ounces whole wheat fettuccine (or pasta
     of choice)
2 tablespoons nutritional yeast
Freshly ground black pepper
Fresh sage leaves, optional

1. Heat 1 tablespoon of the oil in a large skillet over medium-high heat. Add the squash, sprinkle with salt, and cook for 5 minutes. Don't worry if the squash starts to break apart. Add the vegetable stock and cook, still stirring gently until the liquid is almost evaporated, about 7 minutes.

2. Add the onion and season with a little more salt. Cook until the onion begins to soften, 3 minutes. Add the wine, and cook until moisture is almost evaporated and mixture is caramelized. Stir in the maple syrup, vinegar, and sage. Keep warm.

3. Cook the pasta in a pot of boiling salted water until tender, about 10 minutes. Drain the pasta and return it to the hot pot. Add the remaining 1 tablespoon oil, the nutritional yeast, and salt and pepper to taste; toss to combine. Add the vegetable mixture to the pasta and toss again to combine. Serve hot garnished with fresh sage leaves, if using.

kung pao broccoli and tofu

Yield: 4 to 6 servings

The delicately fried tofu pairs well with the broccoli for a generous boost of calcium, protein, and vitamin C. Serve over freshly cooked jasmine or brown rice. For extra heat, add a few shakes of hot red pepper flakes if desired.

Sauce:
4 tablespoons soy sauce
2 tablespoons rice vinegar
2 tablespoons dry sherry
6 tablespoons vegetable stock
1 tablespoon plus 1 teaspoon natural sugar
2 teaspoons brown rice syrup
1 tablespoon plus 1 teaspoon cornstarch
1/2 teaspoon toasted sesame oil, optional

Tofu and Broccoli:
1/3 cup cornstarch
Sea salt

14 ounces extra-firm tofu, drained, pressed, blotted dry, and cut into 1-inch dice
2 tablespoons canola oil, plus more for frying
5 small hot dried chiles
1/2 cup roasted peanuts, plus more for garnish
1 clove garlic, minced
1 teaspoon grated fresh ginger
3 cups small broccoli florets
1 (8-ounce) can sliced water chestnuts, drained
2 scallions, cut into 1/2-inch pieces, plus more for garnish

1. *Sauce:* In a small bowl, combine all the cooking sauce ingredients. Mix well and set aside.

2. *Tofu and Broccoli:* Preheat the oven to 250°F. In a medium bowl, whisk together cornstarch and a couple of pinches of salt. Dredge the tofu in the cornstarch mixture and transfer to a plate.

3. Heat a thin layer of oil in a large skillet over medium-high heat until a drop of water sprinkled on the surface splatters. Add tofu and fry until golden brown all over, about 8 minutes total. Transfer the tofu to a heatproof plate, sprinkle with salt, and keep warm in the oven.

4. Heat 1 tablespoon of the oil in a large skillet or wok over medium heat. Add the chiles and peanuts and stir fry until the chiles begin to char. Do not allow to blacken completely. Remove the chiles and the nuts to a small bowl and set aside.

5. Add the remaining 1 tablespoon oil to the skillet and increase the heat to medium-high. Add the garlic and ginger and quickly stir once. Then add the broccoli, and stir-fry until tender, but still bright green, 3 to 5 minutes. Add the water chestnuts, scallions, and reserved chiles and peanuts and stir just to combine. Add the reserved cooking sauce and cook, stirring continuously, until heated through and nicely thickened. Transfer to a shallow serving bowl or platter, spoon the reserved tofu on top, and garnish with a sprinkling of chopped scallions and peanuts. Serve hot.

sweet potatoes and cannellini beans in sage-butter phyllo crust

Yield: 4 servings

This main dish is special enough for a holiday feast, but simple enough for weeknight meals. Besides, it's too good to only savor once a year.

3 medium sweet potatoes
1 (15.5-ounce) can cannellini beans, rinsed and drained
Zest of one large orange
1 tablespoon nutritional yeast
3 tablespoons fresh minced parsley
1/8 teaspoon garlic powder

1/8 teaspoon onion powder
Sea salt and freshly ground black pepper
1/4 cup vegan butter, melted
2 tablespoons dried rubbed sage
8 sheets phyllo dough, thawed and covered with plastic wrap and a damp towel

1. Preheat the oven to 400°F. Pierce and oil the sweet potatoes and arrange them in a shallow baking pan. Bake until tender, 45 to 60 minutes, depending on the size. Alternatively, you can microwave the potatoes on high until tender, about 6 minutes. Increase the oven temperature to 425°F.

2. Scoop the flesh from sweet potatoes into a medium sized bowl and mash well. Stir in the beans and mash to break up. Stir in the orange zest, nutritional yeast, parsley, garlic powder, onion powder, and salt and pepper to taste. Mix until well combined.

3. In a small bowl, combine the butter and sage. Use a pastry brush to oil the bottom and sides of an 8-inch square metal baking pan. Working with one sheet of phyllo at a time, fold one side down to make about a 9-inch square. Fit it into the bottom of the pan and tuck the edges in so that the dough fits flat, brushing with the sage mixture as you go. Repeat with 3 more sheets of phyllo and the sage mixture.

4. Spoon the filling onto bottom crust and smooth the top. Repeat the crust procedure with the remaining 4 sheets of phyllo, arranging them on top of the filling to make a top crust.

5. Bake for 20 minutes or until golden brown. Cool for 10 minutes, then cut into four squares. Serve warm.

massaman curry tofu with sweet potatoes

Yield: 4 servings

This Thai-inspired curry has been a favorite for a long time. Serve with freshly cooked jasmine rice.

1 large sweet potato, peeled and cut into bite-size chunks
1/4 cup cornstarch
Sea salt
8 ounces extra-firm tofu, pressed, drained, blotted dry and cut into 1-inch cubes
1 tablespoon canola oil
3 tablespoons red curry paste, prepared or home-made
1/2 large yellow onion, cut into 1/2-inch slivers

1 cup fresh or canned pineapple chunks
1 (14-ounce) can unsweetened coconut milk
2 teaspoons vegan fish sauce
1/2 large red bell pepper, cut into 1/4-inch strips
1 1/2 ounces roasted lightly salted peanuts
2 to 3 tablespoons coarsely chopped fresh cilantro
Optional garnish: cilantro sprigs and lime wedges

1. Preheat the oven to 250°F. Steam the sweet potatoes over simmering water until tender, 5 to 7 minutes. Set aside.

2. In a medium bowl, whisk together the cornstarch and 1/4 teaspoon salt. Dredge the tofu in the cornstarch mixture and transfer to a plate.

3. Heat a thin layer of oil in a large skillet over medium-high heat until a drop of water sprinkled on the surface splatters. Add the tofu and fry until golden brown, about 8 minutes. Transfer the tofu to a heatproof plate, sprinkle with salt, and keep warm in the oven.

4. Heat the 1 tablespoon oil in a large skillet or wok over medium-high heat. Add the curry paste and stir fry in the oil for 1 to 2 minutes. And the onion and stir fry another 1 to 2 minutes.

5. Reduce the heat if it is cooking too fast. Add the pineapple and potato and continue stir frying for another 1 to 2 minutes. Stir in the coconut milk and vegan fish sauce and simmer about 5 minutes. Add the red pepper and cook 2 to 3 minutes longer or until the pepper is tender. Stir in the peanuts and cilantro and heat through. Serve the curry in a shallow serving bowl or platter topped with the tofu. Garnish with cilantro and lime wedges, if using.

black-eyed pea and spinach cakes

Yield: 4 servings

These hearty cakes are nutritional powerhouses and a festive way to enjoy your black-eyed peas on New Year's Day or anytime. I like them best served with a colorful Sun-Dried Tomato Tartar Sauce.

Tartar Sauce:
1/3 cup vegan mayonnaise
1 teaspoon fresh lemon juice
3 oil-packed sun-dried tomatoes, finely
    chopped
1 tablespoon capers, drained

Cakes:
4 cups fresh baby spinach
1 (12-ounce) box firm silken tofu
1 cup loosely packed fresh parsley
1 red bell pepper, coarsely chopped

8 scallions, chopped
1 3/4 cups cooked or 1 (15.5-ounce) can
    black-eyed peas, rinsed and drained
1 cup all-purpose flour
1 cup Panko bread crumbs
2 teaspoons baking powder
1/4 teaspoon sweet smoked paprika
3/4 teaspoon fresh thyme leaves or 1/4
    teaspoon dried
Pinch garlic powder
Sea salt and freshly ground black pepper
Canola oil

1. *Tartar Sauce:* In a small bowl, combine the mayo, lemon juice, sun-dried tomatoes, and capers and stir together. Set aside, or cover and refrigerate until needed.

2. *Cakes:* Finely mince the spinach in a food processor and set aside. You should have about 1 cup of spinach.

3. In a food processor, process the tofu until smooth, then scrape into a medium size mixing bowl. In the same food processor, pulse the bell pepper and scallions until finely chopped. Transfer to the bowl with the tofu and add the black-eyed peas, flour, panko, baking powder, paprika, thyme, garlic powder, and salt and pepper to taste. Stir until well combined.

4. In a large skillet, heat the oil over medium-high heat. Use an ice cream scoop to spoon four mounds of the mixture into the oil, flattening the tops of each to make a one-inch thick cake. Cook for 2 minutes or until golden brown. If cakes become dark brown, reduce the heat to medium. Flip and cook 2 more minutes or until golden brown. Serve hot, topped with the reserved tartar sauce.

Side Dishes

"The greatest delight the fields and woods minister is the suggestion of an occult relation between man and the vegetable. I am not alone and unacknowledged. They nod to me and I to them."

— Ralph Waldo Emerson

On the Side...

A delicious side dish is a wonderful way to showcase the essence of a season. Winter's Burgundy-Poached Pears are a show-stopping addition to my family's holiday celebrations. In spring, I enjoy the colors and flavors of Swiss Chard with Hazlenuts. BD's Grilled Summer Squash Boats are simply amazing when it's warm enough to cook under the stars. And when the chill of fall arrives, let the Lemony Parsnips take center stage sprinkled with a warm rosemary-cashew topping. In this chapter, you'll also find recipes for grilling, braising, and roasting all year round.

Side Dishes

asparagus-almond stuffed mushroom caps

Yield: 4 servings

These little bite-size morsels are elegant enough for a sophisticated buffet, but quick and easy enough for dinner on the fly.

1 tablespoon olive oil
1/2 cup chopped onion
4 ounces thin asparagus, cut into 1/2-inch pieces (1 cup)
2 large cloves garlic
Sea salt and freshly ground black pepper
1/3 cup toasted slivered almonds, coarsely chopped

1/4 teaspoon dried marjoram
2 teaspoons natural sugar
2 tablespoons plus 2 teaspoons Creamy White "Cheese" (page 113)
2 teaspoons lemon zest
12 cremini mushroom caps, about 2 inches in diameter, stems removed

1. Preheat the oven to 350°F. Oil a small baking dish and set aside. Heat the oil in a large skillet over medium-high heat. Add the onion and cook, stirring, until it softens and begins to develop some color, 3 to 5 minutes.

2. Add the asparagus, garlic, and salt and pepper to taste. Cook until the asparagus is tender, but still bright green, and the garlic is softened. Add the almonds, marjoram, and sugar, stir to combine, and heat through. Transfer the asparagus mixture to a small bowl. Set aside to cool for a few minutes, then stir in the "cheese" and lemon zest, mixing well.

3. Arrange the mushrooms in the prepared baking dish and divide the filling among them. Bake for 15 minutes or until the mushrooms are tender and filling is hot.

spaghetti squash picatta

Yield: 4 servings

In my pre-vegan days, picatta sauce was always a favorite. Thankfully, it veganizes beautifully. For a refreshing and healthful twist, the picatta sauce is paired with spaghetti squash making it a wonderful side dish that can easily be transformed into a main dish with the addition of cooked or canned cannellini beans.

1 small spaghetti squash (about 1 1/2 pounds)
1 tablespoon olive oil
4 scallions, thinly sliced
2 cloves garlic, minced
1/3 cup Pinot Grigio or other dry white wine
1 tablespoon fresh lemon juice

1 tablespoon vegan butter
1 tablespoon plain soy creamer
1 tablespoon nutritional yeast
1 tablespoon capers, drained
Sea salt and freshly ground black pepper
Optional garnishes: lemon slices, minced parsley, and toasted pine nuts

1. Cook the squash either in the oven or microwave (see note below). For the oven method: Preheat the oven to 375°F. Place the squash, cut side down, in an oiled 3-quart baking dish and roast for 45 minutes. When cool enough to handle, use a fork to scoop out the squash threads, working from the shell to the center. You should end up with about 3 cups cooked squash.

2. Heat the oil in a large skillet over medium-high heat. Add the scallions and garlic, and cook, stirring constantly, for 1 to 2 minutes or until softened. Add the wine and lemon juice and let the liquid cook down for another 1 to 2 minutes. Stir in the butter, soy creamer, nutritional yeast, and capers. Then add the squash and heat, using a fork and a spoon to toss it together with the sauce.

3. Season with salt and pepper to taste. Serve immediately with optional lemon slices, minced parsley, and a few toasted pine nuts.

Note: To microwave the squash, cook one half of the squash at a time by placing each half, cut side down, in a microwave-safe dish with 1/4 inch of water. Cook for 7 to 10 minutes.

red chard with toasted hazelnuts

Yield: 4 servings

Maple syrup and raspberry vinegar lend a delicate flavor to fresh Spring chard. This dish is beautiful as an accompaniment to sautéed tempeh or tofu.

1 bunch red chard, rinsed and well dried
2 tablespoons walnut oil or olive oil,
    divided
2 large cloves garlic, minced
Sea salt

2 tablespoons raspberry vinegar or
    apple cider vinegar
2 tablespoons maple syrup
Freshly ground black pepper
1 tablespoon fresh lemon juice
3 tablespoons chopped toasted hazelnuts

1. Remove and discard the tough stem ends of the chard. Cut off the remaining stems and coarsely chop. Set aside. Roll up each chard leaf lengthwise, jellyroll style, and cut through the resulting cylinder into 1/2-inch slices.

2. Heat 1 tablespoon of the walnut oil in a large skillet over medium heat. Add the garlic and stir continuously until it begins to turn golden. Add the sliced chard stems and a pinch of salt and increase heat to medium-high. Sauté for 2 to 3 minutes. Add the remaining 1 tablespoon oil, and stir well.

3. Add the sliced chard leaves, gently packing them into the skillet and cook them, undisturbed, for 2 to 3 minutes. Using tongs, turn the leaves so that the cooked side is up and sauté for 2 minutes longer. Add the vinegar, maple syrup and black pepper to taste, and cook for 1 minute or until the chard is tender, but not mushy, and a bright-dark green.

4. Quickly transfer the chard to a serving bowl to stop cooking, making sure to include all of the juice and bits of garlic. Squeeze the lemon juice over the top and sprinkle with hazelnuts. Serve hot.

blooming coleslaw

Yield: 4 to 6 servings

In this slaw, the shreds of colorful vegetables are bathed in a creamy dressing with tangy-sweet notes from cider-vinegar, mustard, and maple syrup.

1 scant cup Blooming Platter Mayo
　　(page 91), or your favorite vegan
　　mayonnaise
1/4 cup apple cider vinegar
1/4 cup maple syrup
1 teaspoon prepared mustard

1 teaspoon celery seeds
1/2 teaspoon sea salt
1/8 teaspoon freshly ground black pepper
10 ounces (about 4 cups) shredded red
　　and/or green cabbage
1 cup shredded carrots (about 2 ounces)

Combine all the ingredients except the cabbage and carrots in a medium bowl and stir to mix well. Add the cabbage and carrots and toss together until well combined. Serve immediately or cover and refrigerate for an hour to allow the flavors to marry.

panko-topped cheesy zucchini

Yield: 4 servings

Gently sautéed grated zucchini becomes wonderfully creamy on its own. I up the creaminess factor with a tasty homemade "Swiss Cheese" sauce that contrasts beautifully with the crunchy topping.

2 tablespoons olive oil, divided
2 large zucchini, ends trimmed, skin left
   on, and shredded
1/2 cup Creamy "White Cheese" (page
   113)
1/4 cup Panko bread crumbs

1. Heat 1 tablespoon of the olive oil in a large skillet over medium-high heat. Add the zucchini and sauté until its moisture is released and mostly evaporated. Reduce the heat if necessary to keep the mixture from sticking. Stir in as much of the "cheese" sauce as needed to make a creamy mixture and cook until heated through.

2. Heat the remaining 1 tablespoon oil in a small skillet over medium-high heat. Stir in the bread crumbs and toast, stirring frequently, until the crumbs are golden brown. Transfer the zucchini to a serving bowl and sprinkle with the crumbs. Serve immediately.

bd's grilled summer squash boats

Yield: 4 servings

This simple dish comes courtesy of my friend "BD," Brenda Davidson. In summer, even a steady drizzle won't prevent her from cooking on her wood-burning stove nestled safely in the woods near the lake behind her house. For the less intrepid, BD has kindly provided instructions for preparing the dish on a garden variety grill. A mild mango chutney is ideal for this dish.

2 large yellow summer squash, halved
   lengthwise and seeded
4 teaspoons hot chili sesame oil (or your
   favorite oil)

1/4 cup homemade or prepared mango
   chutney
Sea salt and freshly ground black pepper

Preheat the grill to medium with the lid closed. Arrange the squash, cut side down, on the grill and grill for 5 minutes or until nice grill marks develop. Turn and cook the other side for 5 minutes, or until tender. Transfer to a serving platter and top with a spoonful of chutney. Season to taste with salt and pepper.

grilled eggplant
with tahini-paprika sauce

Yield: 4 servings

This lovely pink sauce is sublime with the grilled eggplant and can also be used over zucchini or yellow summer squash. Paired with the Tunisian Couscous Salad (page 49), it makes a wonderful Summer meal.

1/4 cup tahini
1/4 cup water
1 garlic clove, minced
1 1/2 teaspoons sweet paprika
1 tablespoon minced fresh Italian flat leaf parsley, plus more for garnish

Sea salt and freshly ground black pepper
1/4 teaspoon pomegranate molasses (page 36), optional
1 medium eggplant, cut into 1/2-inch slices
Olive oil

1. In a small bowl, combine the tahini, water, garlic, paprika, the 1 tablespoon parsley, and salt and pepper to taste. Add the pomegranate molasses, if using, and whisk until well blended. Check for seasoning and adjust if necessary. Set aside.

2. Place an oiled and well-seasoned grill pan over medium-high heat. Rub the eggplant slices on both sides with olive oil and sprinkle with salt. Grill until partially tender and nice grill marks have developed, flip, and repeat on the opposite side. The time varies widely depending on the moisture in the eggplant, but it may take as little as 2 to 3 minutes per side. Serve hot or warm drizzled with the reserved sauce and sprinkled with parsley.

quinoa and edamame pilaf with red chard

Yield: 6 to 8 servings

This recipe is the result of a couple of happy accidents and some ingredients I had on hand. Miraculously, I do believe that the combination was spot-on in terms of texture, taste, and color. A sprinkling of nutritional yeast deepened the flavors and a garnish of pea sprouts and lemon zest finished off this hearty and savory summer dish in just the right way.

1 tablespoon olive oil
2 leeks, white part only, thinly sliced, and rinsed and drained
Sea salt
3 cloves garlic, thinly sliced
8 ounces mushrooms, coarsely chopped
3 cups vegetable stock
2 bay leaves
1 1/2 cups uncooked quinoa

1 1/2 cups fresh shelled edamame
1 tablespoon nutritional yeast
3 tablespoons fresh tarragon or 1 tablespoon dried
1 bunch red or green chard, stems removed
Freshly ground black pepper
Garnish: pea sprouts or fresh parsley sprigs, sliced lemon and lemon zest

1. Heat the oil in a 4-quart saucepan over medium-high heat. Add the leeks and a pinch of salt and sauté until the leeks start to soften, 3 to 5 minutes. Add 1 tablespoon of water if they seem too dry. Add the garlic and mushrooms and continue sautéing, until the mushrooms have softened slightly, 3 minutes.

2. Add the stock and bay leaves and bring to a simmer. Stir in the quinoa and simmer, stirring occasionally, for 20 minutes or until the mixture becomes very thick. During the last 5 minutes, stir in the edamame. When the pilaf has finished cooking, turn off the heat and stir in the nutritional yeast, tarragon, and chard. Cover and let it sit for 5 minutes, tossing occasionally, until the chard is wilted. Check for seasoning and add salt and pepper to taste if needed. Garnish as desired and serve hot.

green bean casserole

Yield: 6 servings

This delicious update of a popular holiday casserole is made with fresh green beans, mushrooms, and homemade onion rings. It's great anytime, so don't wait for a holiday to try it.

1/4 cup all-purpose flour, plus more for dredging
Sea salt and freshly ground black pepper
1 medium onion, thinly sliced into rings (about 2 cups)
Olive oil
9 ounces fresh green beans
3 celery ribs, finely chopped
4 scallions, thinly sliced
3 large cloves garlic, thinly sliced
4 ounces fresh white mushrooms, thinly sliced
2 tablespoons nutritional yeast
1 1/2 cups unsweetened soy milk
1/2 teaspoon garlic powder
1/2 teaspoon onion powder

1. Combine 3 to 4 tablespoons of flour in a shallow bowl with salt and pepper to taste. Lightly dredge the onion rings in the flour mixture. Heat a thin layer of oil in a large skillet over medium-high heat. Add the onion rings and fry until lightly browned and crispy, turning once, about 5 minutes.

2. Preheat the oven to 350°F. Oil a 1 1/2 quart casserole dish and set aside. Steam the green beans for 8 minutes or until tender. Set aside.

3. Pour off all but 1 tablespoon oil from the skillet and heat over medium-high heat. Add the celery, scallions, garlic, and salt to taste. Sauté until they begin to soften. Add the mushrooms and sauté until softened, but not mushy, about 5 minutes.

4. In a small bowl, combine the 1/4 cup flour and 1/4 cup of the soy milk, stirring to blend. Set aside.

5. Sprinkle the nutritional yeast on the celery mixture, and stir well to coat. Stir in the flour and soy milk mixture, then add the remaining soy milk and stir well to combine. Add the garlic powder and onion powder. Cook for 3 minutes or until mixture thickens and flour loses its raw taste. Season to taste with salt and pepper. Remove the skillet from the heat and stir in the reserved green beans and about 2/3 cup of the onion rings. Spoon the mixture into the prepared baking dish and bake for 30 minutes. Remove from the oven, gently stir, sprinkle the top with the remaining onion rings and return to the oven for 5 minutes. Serve immediately.

NOTE: To make ahead: Bake the casserole for 30 minutes, cool to room temperature, and store, covered with foil, in the refrigerator. Reheat in a 350°F oven, covered for 15 to 20 minutes or until hot, then top with the onion rings and bake an additional 5 minutes.

caramelized fennel and figs

Yield: 4 servings

The aroma of caramelizing root vegetables captures the essence of fall for me, especially when combined with dried fruit and a nutty oil.

12 dried figs, stemmed and halved
1/2 cup medium-dry sherry
2 tablespoons walnut oil
1 large yellow onion, halved and cut into 1/4-inch slices
2 medium shallots, thinly sliced
1 large fennel bulb, cut into 1/4-inch slices (fronds reserved)

3 garlic cloves, thinly sliced
Sea salt and freshly ground black pepper
1/3 cup fresh orange juice
1 tablespoon balsamic or white balsamic vinegar
Optional garnish: minced fennel fronds

1. Place the figs in a small bowl and cover with the sherry. Set aside.

2. Heat the walnut oil in a large skillet over medium heat. Add the onions, shallots, fennel, and garlic, and season with salt and pepper to taste. Sauté until the vegetables begin to color. Reduce the heat to medium-low and cook for 15 to 20 minutes longer, or until the vegetables are soft and a deep golden color.

3. Add the orange juice and reserved figs and sherry to the skillet, and sauté until heated through. Add the vinegar and stir well to combine. Taste and adjust the seasonings. Serve hot sprinkled with fennel fronds, if using.

braised cabbage, apples, and potatoes

Yield: 4 servings

Nothing says autumn like this cozy braise of cabbage and potatoes with a hint of apple. Serve with the White Bean Sausages, page 110, or other vegan sausages for a fabulous fall meal.

1 tablespoon olive oil
2 small yellow onions, chopped
2 cloves garlic minced
1 teaspoon black or yellow mustard seeds
1 teaspoon caraway seeds
1 teaspoon coriander seeds
1 bay leaf, torn in half
4 cups shredded Napa cabbage
1 pound red-skinned new potatoes, cut into 1-inch pieces

1 large red delicious apple, cored, and cut into 1-inch pieces
1 cup vegetable stock
12 ounces lager beer
1/2 teaspoon Liquid Smoke
1 tablespoon all-purpose flour
1 tablespoon maple syrup
1 tablespoon prepared brown mustard
Sea salt and freshly ground black pepper

1. Heat the oil in a large skillet over medium-high heat. Add onions and garlic, and cook, stirring, until the onions are soft and begin to turn golden, about 7 minutes. Add all the seeds, bay leaf, and cabbage, and cook until the cabbage begins to soften. Add potatoes, apple, stock, beer, and Liquid Smoke and simmer, stirring occasionally, until potatoes and apples are tender, 10 to 12 minutes.

2. Whisk together flour, maple syrup, and mustard and then stir into the vegetable mixture. Simmer, stirring occasionally, for a few minutes or until broth thickens and the raw taste of flour is cooked out. Season to taste with salt and pepper. Serve hot.

acorn squash stuffed
with cheesy swiss chard

Yield: 4 servings

The sweet squash is an ideal foil for the tangy-salty greens, and the light crunch of buttery bread crumbs is the perfect counterpoint.

1 large bunch fresh chard (any kind), rinsed, dried, thick stems removed
2 small acorn squashes, halved cross-wise, seeds and pulp removed
Sea salt
1/2 cup roasted and lightly salted cashews

1/4 cup nutritional yeast
1 tablespoon white miso paste
1/2 cup unsweetened soy milk
2 tablespoons olive oil, divided
4 cloves garlic
1/4 cup Panko breadcrumbs

1. Tear the chard leaves into medium-size pieces and process in a food processor until finely chopped. Set aside.

2. Preheat the oven to 400°F. Sprinkle the cut side of the squash halves lightly with salt and arrange, cut side down, in a shallow baking dish. Add 1/4-inch of water to the baking pan and bake for 25 minutes or until the squash is fork tender, but not mushy. Remove from the oven and carefully transfer each squash to a serving dish, cut side up.

3. While the squash is baking, combine the cashews, nutritional yeast, miso, and soy milk in a food processor. Process until almost smooth, scraping down sides of bowl as necessary. Set aside.

4. Heat 1 tablespoon of the oil in a large skillet over medium-high heat. Add the chard and garlic and sauté for 2 to 3 minutes or until the chard loses its raw taste, lowering heat if necessary to prevent sticking. Stir in the cashew mixture, heat through for 1 minute, then turn off the heat.

5. Heat the remaining 1 tablespoon oil in a small skillet over medium-high heat Add the crumbs and toast, stirring frequently, until golden brown. Fill the cavity in each squash with one-quarter of the filling mixture. Sprinkle the top with crumbs and serve immediately.

lemon-ginger baby bok choy and butternut squash

Yield: 4 servings

A little tangy, a tiny bit sweet, and just a touch spicy, this dish is especially nice paired with sautéed tempeh or seitan. Keep this in mind the next time you have leftover roasted squash or plan ahead and roast some to use in this dish. You can also use a baked sweet potato instead of the squash.

2 cups diced butternut squash
1 tablespoon vegetable oil
1 teaspoon sesame oil
1 tablespoon orange juice
1 1/2 teaspoons soy sauce
1 teaspoon five-spice powder
1 teaspoon light brown sugar
Pinch cayenne pepper

Sea salt
1/2 cup cashew pieces
8 small baby bok choy, halved lengthwise
1/4 cup water
1/2 cup fresh lemon juice
1 teaspoon grated fresh ginger
1/2 teaspoon garlic powder

1. Preheat the oven to 425°F. Spread the squash on a lightly oiled baking sheet and roast until tender, turning once, about 15 minutes total. Set aside.

2. Heat both oils in a large skillet over medium-high heat. Add the orange juice, soy sauce, five-spice powder, brown sugar, cayenne, and salt to taste, and stir until well combined. Add the cashews and cook, stirring frequently, until the cashews are caramelized, 3 minutes. Transfer to a small plate and set aside.

3. Add the bok choy to the same hot skillet and gently sauté until it turns bright green and begins to soften. Add the water, lemon juice, ginger, and garlic powder and cook 3 to 4 minutes until the bok choy is crisp-tender, but still bright green. Add the roasted squash and gently stir to combine while heating through. Season with salt to taste. Stir in the reserved cashew mixture and serve immediately.

lemony parsnips
with rosemary-cashew gremolata

Yield: 4 servings

My love affair with parsnips continues with this incredible lemony dish. The gremolata is such a tasty accompaniment, you might want to double the recipe.

3 large parsnips, peeled, trimmed, and
    cut into 1/2-inch thick slices
1 large yellow onion, halved and sliced
2 large cloves garlic, thinly sliced
3 cups unsweetened soy milk
1/2 teaspoon chili powder
1/2 teaspoon ground cumin
1/2 teaspoon ground coriander

Sea salt
White pepper
1 tablespoon olive oil
2 cloves garlic, minced
1/4 cup fresh rosemary leaves
1/4 cup chopped roasted cashews
2 teaspoons lemon zest
2 tablespoons fresh lemon juice

1. Arrange the parsnip slices in a large skillet, cover with the onion and garlic, and pour in enough soy milk to just barely cover the vegetables. Sprinkle with chili powder, cumin, coriander, and salt and pepper to taste. Heat over medium-high and simmer until the parsnips are tender and soy milk has cooked down and thickly coated the parsnips, about 20 minutes. Stir gently every few minutes. Don't worry if a kind of skim develops.

2. While the parsnips are cooking, make the gremolata. Heat the oil in large skillet over medium-high heat. Add the garlic and rosemary, gently squeezing the rosemary between your fingers to release its fragrance and oils. Cook, stirring constantly, for 2 minutes to soften the garlic and rosemary. Add the cashews and continue cooking, stirring constantly, for 1 to 2 minutes to heat and combine the flavors. Reduce the heat if necessary. Stir in the lemon zest and season with a little salt. Keep warm.

3. Transfer the parsnip mixture to a food processor. Add the lemon juice and process until smooth, scraping down the bowl with a spatula as necessary. Taste the mixture and adjust the seasoning, if needed. To serve, transfer the parsnip puree to a serving bowl and top with the gremolata.

sweet potatoes caribbean

Yield: 4 servings

A childhood favorite inspired this recipe. My mom used to serve mashed sweet potatoes on a ring of pineapple with a marshmallow baked on top. I borrowed that presentation for my tropical take on a Southern staple.

2 large sweet potatoes, peeled and cut into 1-inch dice
2 teaspoons vegan butter
1 tablespoon plus 1 teaspoon peanut butter
1 tablespoon plus 1 teaspoon fresh lime juice
2 tablespoons unsweetened coconut milk

1/4 teaspoon ground cumin
1/4 teaspoon ground coriander
2 teaspoons fresh cilantro, minced
Sea salt and freshly ground black pepper
2 scallions, trimmed, split lengthwise and cut into 1/4-inch pieces
Pineapple rings, for serving (optional)

1. Pour an inch of water into a 4-quart saucepan fitted with a steamer. Cover the pan and bring the water to a simmer. Place the sweet potatoes into the steamer insert, cover loosely, and steam for 10 minutes or until tender.

2. Mash by hand or press the potatoes through a ricer into a medium-size bowl. Add the vegan butter, peanut butter, lime juice, coconut milk, cumin, coriander, and cilantro, and combine well. Taste and adjust the seasoning with salt and pepper, if necessary. Fold in the scallions and mix until well distributed. To serve, transfer to a bowl and serve hot. Alternately, you can scoop the potatoes onto sliced fresh pineapple rings.

two-potato latkes

Yield: 4 servings

Be prepared for rave reviews from all ages – even toddlers – with these golden beauties, made with a combination of sweet potatoes along with the traditional white potatoes. They are perfect for special occasions such as Hanukkah, but simple enough for any day of the week. For an even greater twist on tradition, try adding a pinch of curry powder. I think life is too short to grate potatoes by hand if you don't have to, so consider using the grater attachment of a food processor to make quick work of this task.

1 small sweet potato, peeled and shredded (1 cup packed)
1 Yukon gold potato, peeled and shredded, (1 cup packed)
2 tablespoons grated onion, drained of excess juice
1 tablespoon dried parsley
3 tablespoons cornstarch

Pinch garlic powder
Pinch onion powder
1/2 teaspoon sea salt
Freshly ground black pepper
Canola oil, for frying
Garnish: vegan sour cream and a sprinkling of paprika

1. Preheat the oven to 250°F. Place the shredded potatoes in a large bowl. Add the onion, parsley, cornstarch, onion powder, garlic powder, salt, and pepper to taste. Use a fork to mix until well combined.

2. Heat a thin layer of canola oil in a large skillet over medium-high heat. Place about 1/4 cup of the mixture into the skillet and immediately press firmly with a spatula to flatten. Repeat with more of the mixture, making as many latkes as you can without crowding the pan.

3. After 2 to 3 minutes, or when a crisp surface begins to develop on the bottom, gently loosen the bottom of the latkes with a spatula. If the latkes begin to break up, press them on top with the spatula and cook for another 30 to 45 seconds, pressing frequently, to insure crispiness, and checking to make sure the latkes are not sticking to the skillet. Carefully flip and cook for another 4 minutes.

4. Transfer to a heatproof plate and keep warm in the oven while preparing the remaining latkes. Serve with a small dollop of vegan sour cream and a sprinkling of paprika.

indian cauliflower with black mustard seeds

Yield: 4 servings

This fragrant, Indian-inspired, side dish is simple and delicious. Try using orange cauliflower when making this recipe; it tastes the same as white and it looks beautiful with the black mustard seeds.

2 tablespoons olive oil, divided
1 cup chopped onion
1 head white or orange cauliflower, cut into small florets
2 teaspoons ground coriander
1/2 teaspoon ground turmeric

Sea salt and freshly ground black pepper
1/2 cup water
1 tablespoon vegan butter
1 tablespoon black mustard seeds
1/4 cup chopped fresh cilantro, optional

1. Heat 1 tablespoon of the oil in a large skillet over medium-high heat. Add the onion and cook, stirring frequently, until golden. Add the cauliflower, coriander, turmeric, and salt and pepper to taste. Cook for 2 to 3 minutes. Add the water and simmer until the cauliflower is tender and most of the water is absorbed, 3 to 5 minutes.

2. In a small skillet over medium-high heat, melt butter with the remaining 1 tablespoon olive oil. Add the mustard seeds and cook for 2 minutes.

3. To serve, transfer the cauliflower to a serving platter, drizzle with the mustard seed mixture and sprinkle with cilantro, if using. Serve hot.

curried couscous

Yield: 4 servings

This fluffy side dish is a confetti of gold and orange with ribbons of fresh green spinach. It pairs especially well with Seitan and Kale in Coconut Sauce (page 116).

1 cup vegetable stock
1/2 cup chopped scallions
1/4 cup chopped orange bell pepper
1 cup couscous
1/2 cup golden raisins

1/2 cup packed spinach chiffonade
1 teaspoon curry powder
1 tablespoon olive oil
Sea salt and freshly ground black pepper

Combine the stock, scallions, and bell pepper in a 2-quart saucepan over medium-high heat and bring to a boil. Remove from the heat and stir in the couscous, golden raisins, spinach, and curry powder. Cover and set aside for 5 minutes. Remove the lid and fluff the couscous with a fork while mixing in the olive oil and salt and pepper to taste.

krispy kale

Yield: 4 servings

This flavorful take on kale is positively addictive. To remove the tough stems, fold each kale leaf in half along the stem and use a sharp knife to slice along the edge of the stem to remove. A salad spinner works great for rinsing and drying the kale.

1 bunch kale, tough stems removed,
   rinsed and dried
1 1/2 teaspoons olive oil

1 1/2 teaspoons toasted sesame oil
Sea salt

1. Preheat the oven to 375°F. Tear the kale leaves into 2 to 4 pieces, keeping in mind that they will shrink significantly. Lightly oil a rimmed baking sheet with both oils. Add the kale and toss to coat. Sprinkle lightly with salt and roast for 12 minutes, stirring gently with tongs after 5 minutes and again after 10 minutes. The kale should dry out, brown slightly on the tips of the leaves, and become crispy. Serve immediately.

2. Note: any moisture left on the leaves or an excess of oil will cause the kale to steam rather than crisp up. Leave the kale on the baking sheet until you divide it among individual dinner plates, as transferring it to a serving bowl will cause the bottom leaves to steam.

roasted lemon-coriander sweet potatoes

Yield: 4 servings

I created this dish because some varieties of an old favorite, Terra Chips, are not vegan. I love the lemony note in coriander, so I played it up with fresh lemon zest. My husband said these potatoes would be delicious fried as chips—so I must have come close to my inspiration—but I prefer them roasted.

1 1/2 tablespoons olive oil
2 teaspoons ground coriander
1/2 teaspoon garlic powder
1/2 teaspoon onion powder

1/4 teaspoon sea salt, or to taste
1 pound sweet potatoes, unpeeled, cut
   crosswise into 1/4-inch slices
2 teaspoons lemon zest

Preheat the oven to 450°F. In a small bowl, whisk together the olive oil, coriander, garlic powder, onion powder, and salt. Pour the mixture into a large shallow baking pan. Arrange the sweet potato slices in the oil mixture and then turn over to coat. Roast for 10 minutes. Remove the pan from the oven, flip each slice over, and return the pan to the oven to roast 10 minutes longer. Transfer to a serving platter and sprinkle the zest over the top. Serve immediately.

maple-mustard roasted brussels sprouts

Yield: 4 to 6 servings

When roasted, Brussels sprouts become sweet and caramelized, and they can be every bit as addictive as French fries or popcorn. This dish is delicious plain, but it is extra-special tossed in my light tangy-sweet vinaigrette before the final five minutes of roasting. I like mine really crispy on the outside, but you can shorten the roasting time for less color and crunch.

1 pint Brussels sprouts, rinsed, drained, and sliced in half
2 tablespoons olive oil, divided
Coarse sea salt

1 tablespoon balsamic vinegar
1 tablespoon maple syrup
1/2 teaspoon prepared mustard (I use Grey Poupon)

1. Preheat the oven to 450°F. Pour 1 tablespoon of olive oil into a large roasting pan. Add the Brussels sprouts and salt to taste. Toss to coat. Arrange the Brussels sprouts in a single layer, cut side down, and roast undisturbed for 10 minutes. Stir them gently and roast for 15 minutes longer, stirring occasionally.

2. In a small bowl, combine the remaining 1 tablespoon oil with the vinegar, maple syrup, and mustard. Whisk to blend and set aside.

3. After the 25 minutes of roasting, drizzle the vinaigrette over the Brussels sprouts, stir well to coat, and roast for a final 10 minutes. Transfer immediately to a serving platter or bowl and serve hot.

Note: For less caramelization, roast the Brussels sprouts for only 20 minutes, drizzle them with vinaigrette, and roast for 5 more minutes for a total of 25 minutes.

burgundy poached pears
with rosemary-scented onions

Yield: 6 servings

Last year, when I arrived at my family's house for our annual Christmas holiday visit, I noticed that some handsome Harry & David pears sent by my cousin, Earl, were ripening quickly. I decided to poach them, opting for a savory, rather than a sweet rendition. The result is beautiful, tasty, and festive.

1/4 cup olive oil
1 tablespoon fresh rosemary leaves
1 large lemon, halved, seeded and cut
    into 1/4-inch slices
3 pears, halved lengthwise and cored

3 garlic cloves, peeled and thinly sliced
1 cinnamon stick, halved
Burgundy wine
Sea salt and freshly ground black pepper
1 medium yellow onion, halved and thinly
    sliced

1. Pour the olive oil in a small bowl. Gently crush the rosemary leaves with your fingers as you add them to the bowl. Stir to combine, and set aside.

2. Rub one of the lemon slices over the cut side of the pears. Place the pears, cut side down, into a large skillet. Tuck the lemon slices, garlic slices, and cinnamon sticks between the pears. Add enough wine to come halfway up the sides of the pears and then season with salt and pepper.

3. Turn the heat to medium-high and bring the wine to a simmer. Poach the pears for 7 minutes and then gently turn each one and poach for another 7 minutes or until tender, but not falling apart. (Note: very firm or large pears may take longer to poach.)

4. Heat 1 tablespoon of the reserved rosemary oil in a large skillet over medium-high heat. Add the onion and sauté for 5 minutes, or until soft and golden, adding more of the oil if needed.

5. To serve, transfer the pears and onions to a serving platter. Drizzle with the remaining oil mixture and a sprinkling of salt and pepper. Serve hot, warm, or room temperature.

grilled butternut squash
with white beans and olivada

Yield: 4 to 6 servings

This dish was inspired by a delicious white bean and olivada combination that I was served in a restaurant and a bottle of truffle oil that I glimpsed in my pantry. The deep savory flavor of the bean and olive paste provides a dramatic contrast to the sweetness of the grilled winter squash.

1 medium butternut squash, halved lengthwise, seeds and pulp removed
Olive oil
Sea salt
1 (15-ounce) can cannellini beans, rinsed and drained

2 tablespoons olivada, (page 145) or purchased
4 cloves roasted garlic (page 145), minced
2 teaspoons minced fresh Italian flat leaf parsley, plus more for garnish
Freshly ground black pepper
Truffle oil, optional

1. Cut the squash halves into 1/2-inch thick slices. Remove the skin from the squash slices with a paring knife and discard. Heat a well-oiled and seasoned grill pan over medium-high. Rub the squash slices liberally with oil, sprinkle with salt, and arrange in the hot grill pan. Grill on each side for 3 to 5 minutes or until the squash is tender and has developed nice grill marks. Adjust heat, if necessary to prevent it from cooking too quickly.

2. Heat 1 tablespoon of the olive oil in a large skillet over medium-high heat. Add the beans and sauté until the moisture begins to evaporate, 3 minutes. Stir in the olivada and garlic and heat through. Remove the pan from the heat and stir in the parsley. Season to taste with salt and pepper.

3. To serve, arrange 3 to 5 squash slices in a fan-shape on each plate and top each portion with a small scoop of beans. Drizzle liberally with truffle oil, if using, or olive oil and garnish with more parsley. Serve immediately.

olivada

Yield: 3/4 cup

Also known as black olive paste, this luxurious paste is versatile and can be used to add a rich olive flavor to a number of dishes. Pine nuts are used in this recipe but another variety of nuts, such as pistachios, walnuts, or almonds, may be substituted.

1 (6-ounce) can pitted brine-cured
    black olives, drained
2 tablespoons pine nuts
2 tablespoons extra-virgin olive oil
1/4 cup packed flat leaf parsley leaves

1 1/2 teaspoons fresh oregano leaves or
    1/2 teaspoon dried
3/4 teaspoon fresh thyme leaves or 1/4
    teaspoon dried
Sea salt and freshly ground black pepper

In a food processor, combine the olives, nuts, oil, parsley, oregano, thyme, and salt and pepper to taste. Process until smooth, scraping down sides as necessary. Scrape the paste into a small bowl. Cover, and refrigerate until serving time.

Roasted Garlic

1 garlic bulb
olive oil

Preheat the oven to 400°F. Remove the excess papery skin from the outside of the garlic bulb. Trim away 1/4-inch of the top, exposing the tips of the individual cloves. Rub the bulb liberally with oil and then enclose in a foil pouch. Roast for 30 to 35 minutes or until the garlic cloves are soft and golden. Open the foil and set aside to allow the garlic to cool. Remove the garlic from the skin by squeezing gently at the base of each clove. The roasted garlic is now ready to use in recipes and can be stored in a tightly covered container in the refrigerator.

Desserts

> "Life is uncertain. Eat dessert first."
> — Ernestine Ulmer

Sweet Things...

Every season brings new opportunities to enjoy delicious desserts. I adore chocolate, especially when paired with flavors that complement its many complex notes. In the spring, I like to create a Chocolate-Covered Strawberry Tart using early berries. For a summer treat, try my prizewinning Macadamia Shortbread Tart with Lemon Mousse. It's covered with fresh berries and paired with a buttery shortbread crust. In the fall, try my Baked Apples Baklava. It's so warming on a crisp day – as good for breakfast as it is for dessert. The Chocolate-Orange Mousse brightens any winter evening with rich bittersweet chocolate and its perfect counterpoint: juicy oranges.

Desserts

chocolate carrot cake

Yield: 8 servings

When my friend Anne Wolcott raved about the chocolate carrot cake she served at her wedding, "mouth watering" was not the first thought that came to mind. I adore both chocolate and fresh spring carrots, but I didn't think they could be happily married. However, Nora Pouillon of the eponymous Restaurant Nora in Washington, D.C., knew exactly what she was doing as culinary match-maker. Her cake inspired my vegan version.

Cake:
1 cup soy milk
1 tablespoon apple cider vinegar
1 cup unbleached all-purpose flour
3/4 cup plus 2 tablespoons natural sugar
1/2 cup unsweetened cocoa powder
1 teaspoon ground cinnamon
1/2 teaspoon baking powder
1 teaspoon baking soda
1/4 teaspoon sea salt

1/3 cup walnut oil or canola oil
1/2 teaspoon vanilla extract
1 1/2 cups grated carrots
Ganache:
9 ounces vegan semi-sweet chocolate
    chips
1/2 cup vegan sour cream
Garnish:
Halved or chopped pecans or walnuts

1. *Cake:* Preheat the oven to 350°F. Grease and flour a 9-inch round cake pan.

2. In a small bowl, whisk together the soy milk and vinegar. Set aside to curdle, whisking a couple of times. In a large bowl, whisk together the flour, sugar, cocoa powder, cinnamon, baking powder, baking soda, and salt. Make a well in the center of the dry ingredients and add the soy milk mixture, walnut oil, and vanilla. Stir until all ingredients are well combined and no lumps remain. Stir in the carrots.

3. Transfer the batter to the prepared pan and bake for 25 to 30 minutes or until a wooden pick inserted in the center comes out clean. Let the cake cool in the pan on a wire rack for 10 minutes. Run a knife around the side and then invert onto the rack to cool completely, covered with a kitchen towel. Transfer to a serving platter.

4. *Ganache:* In a double-boiler, heat the chocolate chips until melted, stirring frequently until smooth. Alternatively, you may heat them in a microwave-safe bowl at 20 to 30 second intervals in the microwave, whisking after each. Remove the pan from the heat and quickly whisk in the sour cream.

5. *To assemble:* Frost the top of the cake with the ganache, allowing some to cascade over the edges. Garnish with pecans or walnuts.

coffee gelée
with strawberries and crème anglaise

Yield: 4 servings

A centuries-old dessert gets a spring make-over. Use your choice of regular or decaffeinated coffee, flavored or not. I like to make this in individual (1/2 cup) baking or gelatin molds, but you can make it in one larger (2 cup) mold if you prefer.

1 3/4 cups brewed coffee
1/4 cup natural sugar
1 tablespoon plus 1 teaspoon agar flakes
1/4 cup soy creamer

1/2 teaspoon vanilla
8 strawberries, hulled and sliced
Crème Anglaise (recipe follows)

1. Spray a 2-cup gelatin or baking mold or 4 (1/2-cup) molds with nonstick spray and set aside. Combine the coffee, sugar, and agar in a 2-quart saucepan over medium-high heat. Whisk the mixture well and bring it to a boil. Reduce the heat to a vigorous simmer and cook for 5 minutes, whisking occasionally to insure that the agar has dissolved.

2. Remove the pan from the heat, stir in the soy creamer and the vanilla until completely incorporated, and cool the mixture slightly. Carefully pour it into the prepared mold and allow it to cool to room temperature. Cover and chill completely, several hours or overnight.

3. To remove from the mold, invert it onto a serving plate, tapping and squeezing the mold lightly. If it doesn't come out, use your finger to press gently around the top edge of the gelee to break its seal and invert it onto a plate. Alternatively, dip the mold very quickly in a small bowl of warm water and squeeze the mold gently as you invert it. Serve immediately with sliced strawberries in a pool of Crème Anglaise. (If allowed to sit, the gelee will produce liquid around the base. If that occurs, just blot it with a paper towel.)

Variation: Green Tea Gelée

Follow the recipe for Coffee Gelee, substituting strongly brewed tea for the coffee. Omit the soy creamer and vanilla, instead adding 2 tablespoons of lemon juice after removing the mixture from the heat.

---

crème anglaise

With a flavor and silky consistency similar to luscious semi-melted ice cream, Crème Anglaise is a beautiful addition to many desserts and is especially good served over fresh berries. Note: Bring any leftovers to room temperature before serving, as reheating the mixture could cause it to break.

1 3/4 cup plus 1/4 cup soy creamer
1/4 cup plus 1 tablespoon natural sugar
2 tablespoons arrowroot powder

1/2 teaspoon vanilla extract
2 tablespoons plain soy milk (optional)

In a 1-quart saucepan over medium-high, heat the 1 3/4 cup soy creamer and sugar to a gentle boil. Meanwhile, in a small bowl, whisk together the 1/4 cup soy creamer and the arrowroot powder. Remove the pan from the heat as soon as it reaches a boil and stir in the arrowroot mixture. The Crème Anglaise will thicken immediately. Stir in vanilla extract and, if desired, add the soy milk for a thinner sauce. Cool it almost to room temperature before serving.

mango-coconut cream sorbet

Yield: about 1 quart

On my husband's and my twentieth anniversary trip to Paris, "*mangue*" sorbet at a popular little establishment on the Isle St. Louis became my *de rigueur* after-dinner treat. I think my stateside version made with Cream of Coconut is even *plus délicieux.*

1 (15-ounce) can Cream of Coconut
    (I use use Coco Lopez brand "lite")
2 fresh ripe mangoes, pitted and peeled
Juice of 2 fresh limes

Combine all ingredients in a food processor. Process until completely smooth, scraping down the sides of the bowl as necessary. Transfer the mixture to a medium bowl. Cover and chill for 3 hours or overnight. Freeze the mixture in an ice cream maker according to manufacturer's directions.

chocolate-covered strawberry tart

Yield: 8 servings

I served this beautiful tart with afternoon tea to one of my former students, Maddie Jonson, and her mother, Suzanne. With its bold graphic pattern of chocolate drizzled over concentric rings of plump juicy strawberries, it was almost too pretty to eat. Almost.

Ganache:
1/2 cup soy creamer
9 ounces vegan semi-sweet chocolate
    chips
Pinch sea salt

Crust:
1 1/2 cups all-purpose flour
3 tablespoons unsweetened cocoa
    powder
6 tablespoons natural sugar
1 teaspoon sea salt
1/2 cup plus 1 tablespoon canola oil

2 tablespoons soy milk

Custard Filling:
6 ounces extra-firm silken tofu
1/4 cup granulated sugar
2 1/2 tablespoons cornstarch
1/2 cup soy milk
1/2 teaspoon almond extract
1 tablespoon Amaretto (optional)

To assemble:
13 fresh strawberries, rinsed, hulls removed,
    12 of them halved lengthwise
Confectioners' sugar, optional

1. *Ganache:* In a small saucepan over medium-high, heat soy creamer until bubbles start to appear around the edges. (You may instead heat it in a microwave-safe bowl for 20 second intervals in the microwave.) Remove from heat and quickly whisk in chocolate chips until satiny smooth. Cool to room temperature, whisking occasionally.

2. *Crust:* Preheat the oven to 400°F. In a medium bowl, mix the flour, cocoa powder, sugar, and salt. Make a well in the center, and add the oil and soy milk. Stir until all of the liquid is absorbed. Transfer to a fluted tart crust pan with a removable bottom and press the crust evenly into the bottom and sides. Bake for 15 minutes. Transfer the pan to a wire rack and cool for about 3 minutes. Reduce oven temperature to 350°F.

3. *Custard Filling:* Combine all the ingredients in a food processor and process until smooth, scraping down the sides of the bowl as necessary.

4. *To assemble:* Spread the custard into the prepared crust, smoothing the top with a wooden spoon or spatula. Bake 20 minutes. Transfer to a wire rack and cool to room temperature. Arrange the berry halves in concentric circles on the surface of the custard, placing the whole berry in the center. Drizzle the ganache in concentric circles, over the berries from the tip of a spoon or from a plastic squirt bottle. Cover and chill for 2 to 3 hours or longer.

5. To serve, remove the sides from the tart pan and place the tart on a serving platter. Garnish the tart with an optional dusting of confectioners' sugar.

Chantilly "Whipped Cream"

Chantilly means "sweetened whipped cream," and you can use it all year round on berries, cakes, puddings, parfaits, and any time you'd like a dollop of whipped cream to make a dessert special.

- 2 cups raw unsalted cashew pieces, divided
- 2 cups water, divided
- 6 tablespoons confectioners' sugar
- 2 tablespoons lemon juice
- 1/2 teaspoon vanilla extract

Place 1 cup of the cashews in a medium bowl and cover with one cup of the water. Cover the bowl and refrigerate overnight. Drain and rinse the cashews in a colander. Transfer the cashews to a food processor, add the remaining one cup of water, and process until creamy, scraping down the sides of the bowl as necessary with a rubber spatula. Add the remaining cup of cashews and process another few minutes, or until thick and creamy, again scraping down the sides of bowl as necessary. The mixture should have enough body to hold a peak. Add the confectioners' sugar, lemon juice, and vanilla extract and process until combined. Taste and adjust flavoring if necessary.

Transfer the cream into an airtight container and chill it for at least an hour before using. Store covered in the refrigerator.

Yield: about 2 cups

cherry-almond clafouti cake

Yield: 8 servings

To me, this cake is the ideal balance of custardy tenderness and enough body to slice neatly. The consistency is more firm than traditional clafouti, which is why I call it a Clafouti Cake. The almond flavor is less intense and even more appealing when the cake is allowed to cool to room temperature. Instead of cherries, you may substitute 2 cups of another fruit such as sliced fresh summer peaches or apricots.

1 (12-ounce) box firm silken tofu
1 (8-ounce) can almond paste, broken up into small pieces
1/2 cup natural sugar, plus more for sprinkling

1 teaspoon vanilla extract
1/2 teaspoon sea salt
1 cup self-rising flour
1 pint fresh cherries, pitted and halved
Confectioners' sugar, optional

1. Preheat the oven to 350°F. Thoroughly grease and flour a large (10-inch) ovenproof skillet. Place the tofu, almond paste, sugar, vanilla, and salt in a food processor. Process until smooth, scraping down the sides of the bowl as necessary. Add the flour and pulse until combined. Scrape the mixture into the prepared skillet and smooth the top. Cover the surface with the cherries.

2. Sprinkle with the remaining tablespoon of sugar. Bake for 30 minutes, or until a wooden pick inserted in the center and near the side comes out clean. Run a knife around the edge of the pan and cool the cake to room temperature. Sprinkle the top with confectioners' sugar, if desired. To serve, cut the cake into wedges.

lemon verbena shortbread cookies

Yield: about 36 cookies

In my garden is a prolific Lemon Verbena plant, and I love its earthy, lemon flavor. Verbena leaves can be pulsed with sugar in a food processor before proceeding with any recipe for baked goods calling for sugar. And, indeed, the lovely leaves work beautifully in these shortbread cookies.

1 cup confectioners' sugar, plus more for coating
1 cup lemon verbena leaves
3/4 cup vegan butter, room temperature
1 to 2 tablespoons cold water

1 tablespoon vanilla extract
1 3/4 cup plus 2 tablespoons unbleached all-purpose flour
2 tablespoons cornstarch

1. Combine the sugar and lemon verbena leaves in a food processor and process until the leaves are finely minced. Add the vegan butter, water, vanilla, flour, and cornstarch, and pulse until the dough begins to come together. Scrape the sides of the bowl with a spatula, and pulse again until the dough forms a ball. The dough should be quite stiff, but not dry and crumbly. Divide the dough into two halves and arrange each one in the center of a square of waxed or parchment paper. With floured fingers, form each into a 1 1/2 inch diameter log, tapping the ends to flatten them. Roll the logs smoothly in waxed paper or parchment paper, place them on a baking sheet, and chill them for at least an hour.

2. When ready to bake the cookies, preheat the oven to 350°F. Line two baking sheets with Silpat or parchment paper. Unroll the logs and slice them on a slight diagonal into 1/4-inch wide cookies. Place the cookies on the prepared baking sheets about 1 inch apart. Bake them until they are barely golden, about 15 minutes. Transfer the cookies to a rack to cool slightly, about 8 to 10 minutes. While still warm, place the cookies, a few at a time, in a bag filled with about 2/3 cup confectioners' sugar; gently shake to coat. Store leftover cookies in an airtight container in the refrigerator.

macadamia shortbread tart
with lemon mousse and fresh berries

Yield: 8 servings

The vegetarian version of this refreshing dessert won one of two top monthly prizes for "Lemon Desserts" in the January 2003 *Better Homes & Gardens*. This vegan iteration is even better with the addition of glistening red summer raspberries nestled into a citrus cream.

Shortbread Tart:
1/2 cup vegan butter
1/2 cup confectioners' sugar
3/4 cup unbleached all-purpose flour
2 tablespoons yellow cornmeal (regular or self-rising)
2 tablespoons cornstarch
6 tablespoons finely chopped toasted macadamias or other nuts, optional

Lemon Mousse:
3/4 cup sugar
1/4 cup cornstarch
1 cup soy milk

Pinch sea salt
1/4 teaspoon vanilla extract
1/8 teaspoon almond extract
6 ounces extra-firm silken tofu (3/4 cup)
1/4 cup fresh lemon juice
Zest of one large lemon
Chantilly Whipped Cream (page 153) or your favorite whipped topping
1/2 pint of blackberries, blueberries or raspberries
Optional garnish: sprigs of fresh mint; lemon slices

1. *Shortbread Tart:* Grease a baking sheet or line it with Silpat. Preheat the oven to 325°F.

2. In an electric mixer, cream together the butter and sugar. With mixer on low, mix in flour, cornmeal, and cornstarch just until combined. Avoid overbeating. Mix in the nuts, if using, until well distributed. The dough should be very stiff. If it feels soft, gather into a ball, wrap in plastic and refrigerate for 30 minutes.

3. With floured fingers, press the dough into an 8-inch circle on the prepared baking sheet. Prick the surface all over with a fork. Bake the crust for 18 to 20 minutes or until edges are barely browned. Avoid overbaking, as the shortbread will break rather than slice when you try to cut it.

4. Remove the pan from the oven to a wire rack and cool the shortbread for 10 minutes. Carefully remove it from the pan and cool completely on the wire rack. Transfer the crust to a serving platter, cover tightly, and set it aside until the mousse is chilled.

5. *Lemon Mousse:* In a medium saucepan, whisk together the sugar and cornstarch.

Add the soy milk and salt, and whisk until smooth. Place the pan over medium-high heat and cook the mixture, stirring continually, until thick. Reduce the heat if necessary to prevent sticking and scorching. Transfer the mixture to a heatproof bowl, and place it in a larger bowl filled with ice water. Cool the custard, stirring occasionally, for about 30 minutes.

6. Combine the tofu and lemon juice in a food processor and process until smooth, scraping down the sides of the bowl as necessary. Add the custard mixture and continue processing until completely incorporated. Add the zest and pulse to distribute. Transfer the mixture to a bowl and chill, covered, for 1 to 2 hours.

7. **To assemble:** When the mousse is thoroughly chilled, spread it over the surface of the shortbread, stopping 1/2-inch from the edge. Cover and chill the tart overnight. Just before serving, decorate the top with berries and garnish with the whipped cream and optional sprigs of mint or lemon slices.

bourbon-broiled peaches

Yield: 4 servings

Where we live in coastal Virginia, peaches are one of the glories of summer. It is hard to beat fresh peaches when eaten at the height of summer, fuzz and all, juice dripping down one's chin. This preparation pays homage to the essence of the peach with the distinctive flavor of bourbon. It's irresistible with the Peaches-n-Cream Ice Cream, or to save time, a store-bought vegan vanilla ice cream may be substituted.

2 peaches, rinsed, halved and pitted
2 tablespoons bourbon
4 teaspoons natural sugar

Pinch sea salt
4 scoops Peaches-n-Cream Ice Cream
   (recipe follows), or your favorite vegan
   vanilla ice cream (optional)

1. Position the oven rack on the top shelf of your oven and preheat the broiler. Place the peach halves, cut side up, in a small, shallow heat-proof dish. Brush them with the bourbon. Sprinkle each half with a teaspoon of sugar and a tiny pinch of salt. Broil for about 5 minutes to heat them through and melt the sugar. Watch them carefully to prevent scorching.

2. To serve, arrange broiled peach halves in shallow dessert bowls and top each with one scoop of the ice cream, if using.

peaches-n-cream ice cream

Yield: 1 quart

Make this delicious ice cream the day before you plan to serve it.

1 very large ripe peach, halved, pitted,
    skin left on
Juice of one small lemon
1/2 cup unsweetened soy milk, divided
1 cup plain soy creamer
3/4 cup natural sugar
1 large vanilla bean pod, split length-
    wise, and seeds scraped out with the
    tip of a paring knife

2 tablespoons arrowroot powder
3 tablespoons pure peach preserves,
    optional
1/2 teaspoon vanilla extract (or more to
    taste)
1 1/2 cups vegan sour cream

1. Cut the peach into chunks and add to a food processor with the lemon juice. Process until it is a smooth puree. Set aside.

2. In a 1-quart saucepan, combine 1/4 cup soy milk, soy creamer, sugar, and vanilla seeds over medium heat and bring just to a boil.

3. In a small bowl, whisk the remaining 1/4 cup soy milk with the arrowroot powder until smooth. When the soy creamer mixture just reaches a boil, remove the pan quickly from the heat and whisk in the soy milk-arrowroot mixture until very smooth and thickened. Stir in the vanilla extract followed by the reserved peach mixture, peach preserves, if using, and vanilla extract. Allow the mixture to cool to room temperature. Whisk if lumps remain and/or press the mixture through a sieve. Cover the mixture and refrigerate it at least three hours or overnight; then whisk in the sour cream.

4. Freeze the ice cream according to your ice cream maker's manufacturer's directions. Scrape the finished ice cream into an airtight container and store in the freezer. Allow the ice cream to "ripen" and further set up before serving, if desired.

chocolate-plum clafouti cake

Yield: 8 servings

A big beautiful purple plum inspired this not-too-sweet dessert that is as luscious as it is lovely to behold. A little firmer than a traditional clafouti, but still a little custardy, this clafouti cake slices well.

1 (12-ounce) box firm silken tofu
1 (8-ounce) can almond paste, broken up into small pieces
1/2 cup plus 1 tablespoon natural sugar, plus more for sprinkling
2 tablespoons canola oil
1/4 cup plus 2 tablespoons cocoa powder

1 teaspoon vanilla extract
3/4 teaspoon sea salt
1 cup self-rising flour
1 large ripe purple plum, halved, pitted, and cut into 16 slices
Confectioners' sugar, optional

1. Preheat the oven to 350°F. Thoroughly grease and flour a 10-inch ovenproof skillet.

2. Combine the tofu, almond paste, 1/2 cup sugar, canola oil, cocoa powder, vanilla, and salt in a food processor and process until smooth, scraping down the sides of the bowl as necessary. Add the flour and pulse just until combined. Scrape the mixture into the prepared skillet and lightly smooth the top.

3. Arrange the plum slices on the top surface in the shape of a pinwheel. Sprinkle with the remaining 1 tablespoon sugar, and bake about 30 minutes or until a wooden pick inserted in the center and near the side comes out clean or with a few moist crumbs. Run a knife around the edge of the pan and cool the cake to room temperature. Sprinkle the top with confectioners' sugar, if desired. To serve, cut the cake into wedges.

apple-brandy cake
with pecan-praline frosting

Yield: 8 servings

This moist cake will be a hit made with your garden variety brandy. Make it with apple brandy, and it will have everyone "buzzing" about the secret ingredient.

1 cup soy milk
2 tablespoons apple cider vinegar, divided
2 medium sweet-tart apples, sliced
1 1/2 cups unbleached all-purpose flour
1/4 cup whole-wheat flour
3/4 cup natural sugar
Pinch sea salt
1 tablespoon baking powder

1/2 teaspoon ground cinnamon
1/4 teaspoon ground nutmeg
1/8 teaspoon ground cloves
1/4 cup canola oil
3 tablespoons apple brandy or brandy, divided
1/4 teaspoon vanilla extract
1 teaspoon baking soda
Pecan-Praline Frosting (recipe follows)

1. Preheat the oven to 350°F. Grease and flour a 9-inch cake pan and set aside.

2. In a medium bowl, whisk together the soy milk and 1 tablespoon of the apple cider vinegar and set aside to curdle.

3. In a food processor, process apple until it is chopped coarse-fine, about 20 quick pulses. Set aside.

4. In a large bowl, whisk together both flours, the sugar, salt, baking powder, cinnamon, nutmeg, and cloves. Whisk the canola oil, 2 tablespoons of the brandy and vanilla into the soy milk mixture.

5. Make a well in the center of the dry ingredients and pour the wet ingredients into it. Stir the mixture with a wooden spoon to incorporate the wet into the dry ingredients. When the two are partially combined, add the apple and stir until all of the ingredients are well combined.

6. In a small bowl, whisk the remaining 1 tablespoon vinegar with the baking soda. When it fizzes up, incorporate it well into the batter.

7. Transfer the mixture to the prepared cake pan and gently smooth the top. Bake for 25 to 30 minutes or until the cake pulls away from the sides of the pan, a wooden pick inserted in the center of the cake comes out clean, and the top of the cake is golden brown and fairly firm.

8. Remove the pan from the oven and allow the cake to cool in the pan for 10 min-

utes. Run a knife around the sides of the pan and invert the cake onto a wire rack to cool. While the cake is still warm, use a pastry brush to apply the remaining 1 tablespoon of brandy to the top surface. Cool the cake completely.

9. Spread the top with Pecan-Praline Frosting as soon as the frosting is ready and while it is still warm, allowing some to cascade over the edges. Serve immediately or tightly cover and refrigerate until serving time. Remove the cake from the refrigerator at least 30 minutes before serving time.

pecan-praline frosting

Yield: about 1 1/2 cups

3 tablespoons vegan butter
3/4 cup firmly packed brown sugar
1/4 cup soy creamer
1 1/2 tablespoons apple brandy or brandy

1/4 teaspoon vanilla extract
1/8 teaspoon almond extract
1 cup plus 4 tablespoons confectioners' sugar
3/4 cup chopped toasted pecans

In a 4-quart saucepan over medium-high heat, bring the vegan butter, brown sugar, soy creamer, and apple brandy to a gentle boil. Boil the mixture gently for 1 minute, stirring often. Remove the pan from the heat and stir in the vanilla and almond extracts. Whisk in the confectioners' sugar until smooth. Stir in pecans and continue stirring gently for 3 to 5 minutes or until the mixture begins to cool, thicken, and take on a caramel color.

baked apples baklava with cider sauce

Yield: 4 servings

Baked apples are one of the wonders of autumn. In this dessert, tender stuffed apple halves are wrapped up like a beautiful package in buttery phyllo dough. They are as scrumptious for breakfast or brunch as they are for dessert.

Apples:
1/2 cup finely chopped walnuts
1 tablespoon natural sugar
1/4 teaspoon apple pie spice
2 teaspoons agave nectar
2 large McIntosh or other sweet-tart red
    apples, stemmed
Juice of one lemon
1/4 cup vegan butter
1/4 cup olive oil
1 teaspoon natural sugar

16 sheets phyllo dough, thawed
Cider Sauce:
3/4 cup apple cider
3/4 cup sugar
1/2 cup agave nectar
1 tablespoon lemon juice
1 cinnamon stick, halved

Optional Garnish:
Cinnamon stick halves
Chopped walnuts

1. *Apples:* Preheat the oven to 350°F. In a small bowl, combine the walnuts, sugar, apple pie spice, and agave nectar and set aside. Cut the apples in half lengthwise. Using a melon baller, remove the core of the apples in two scoops to make a generous void for the filling. Rub the cut surface of the apples with lemon juice. Press one-fourth of walnut filling into each hollowed out void.

2. Combine the vegan butter and olive oil in a small bowl. Unroll the phyllo dough and cover with plastic wrap and a damp towel. Remove one sheet of dough to a flat work surface and brush lightly with butter-oil mixture. Repeat with three more sheets, stacking them.

3. Place the apple half, filling side up, in the center of the stacked phyllo. Bring up one corner of the dough over the filling, then the opposite corner. Repeat with the remaining corners, smoothing as you go, to make a tight package.

4. Brush on a little more butter-oil mixture and place the apples, flat side down, on a baking sheet or stone. Brush the top with a little more of the butter-oil mixture, smoothing down the edges of the dough. Repeat with remaining apple halves, filling and dough. Sprinkle each with 1/4 teaspoon of sugar. Bake for 30 minutes.

5. *Cider Sauce:* In a 1 quart saucepan, combine all ingredients. Bring to a boil, reduce heat to medium and simmer 15 minutes. Cool slightly to serve. Remove the cinnamon stick halves before serving or use them as two of the garnishes.

6. *To assemble:* Arrange the baked apples on dessert plates drizzled with the Cider Sauce and garnished with cinnamon sticks and walnuts, if using.

cranberry crumble
with rosemary-pecan streusel

Yield: 8 servings

This is a favorite family Thanksgiving dessert. It is sophisticated, yet still appealingly homespun. It is especially delicious served with the Cinnamon Stick-Vanilla Bean Ice Cream (page 171).

Filling:
1 12-ounce bag fresh cranberries (see note below)
1 cup water
1 cup raw sugar
1/2 teaspoon ground cinnamon
2 tablespoons brandy
1 tablespoon orange zest

Crust and Crumble:
1 cup packed light brown sugar

1/2 cup unbleached all-purpose flour
1/2 cup whole-wheat flour
1 cup old fashioned oats, uncooked
1/2 teaspoon ground cinnamon
1/4 teaspoon baking powder
1/4 teaspoon baking soda
1/4 teaspoon salt
1 tablespoon minced fresh rosemary leaves
1/2 cup canola oil
1/2 cup coarsely chopped pecans

1. *Filling:* In a 2-quart saucepan, mix together cranberries, water, sugar, and cinnamon. Bring the mixture to a boil, reduce the heat and simmer, uncovered, for 10 minutes, stirring occasionally. Cool. Stir in brandy and orange zest. Set aside.

2. *Crust and Crumble:* Preheat the oven to 350°F. In a medium bowl, combine all the ingredients except the oil and pecans, and mix with a fork. Drizzle on the oil and mix with the fork until crumbly. Spoon half of this mixture into a 9-inch glass or ceramic deep dish pie pan. Pour the filling over the crust to cover. Mix the pecans with the remaining pastry mixture and crumble evenly over the filling. Bake for 30 to 35 minutes or until nicely browned. Cool slightly before serving.

Note: During months when cranberries aren't widely available, you may substitute two cans of whole berry cranberry sauce for the bag of cranberries, water and sugar. No need to heat them; simply pour them into a bowl and stir in remaining ingredients.

pumpkin-apple butter cheesecake pie

Yield: 8 servings

My niece, Gabriella, and I created this recipe together as part of our Thanksgiving feast. The pie is wonderful and, with the addition of Maple Glazed Nuts (page 165), it is truly something to be thankful for!

Cheesecake Pie:
1 (12-ounce) box firm silken tofu
4 ounces vegan cream cheese
1/3 cup all-purpose flour
1/2 cup canned solid-pack pumpkin
   or pumpkin puree, pressed and
   drained
1/2 cup apple butter
1/2 cup soy-milk
1/2 cup natural sugar

1 teaspoon vanilla extract
1 vegan graham cracker crust

Sour Cream Topping:
1 cup vegan sour cream
3 tablespoons natural sugar
1/4 teaspoon vanilla extract

Garnishes:
Chantilly "Whipped Cream" (page 153), or
   your favorite vegan whipped topping
Maple Glazed Nuts (recipe follows)

1. *Cheesecake Pie:* Preheat the oven to 350°F. In a food processor, combine the tofu, cream cheese, flour, pumpkin, apple butter, soy milk, sugar, and vanilla. Process until smooth and well combined, scraping down the sides of the bowl as necessary. Transfer the mixture to the crust and bake for 45 minutes. Remove the cheesecake from the oven to a wire rack to cool.

2. *Sour Cream Topping:* In a small bowl, whisk together all ingredients until completely combined.

3. *To assemble:* Spread the topping evenly over the surface of the cheesecake and return it to the oven for 10 minutes. Remove the cheesecake from the oven to a wire rack, cool it completely, cover it tightly and refrigerate for several hours or overnight.

4. *To serve:* Spread the top with the whipped cream or your favorite vegan whipped topping, sprinkle with Maple Glazed Nuts, and serve immediately. If not serving right away, sprinkle the nuts on the top just before serving.

maple glazed nuts

Yield: 8 servings

1 cup pecans or walnuts
Pinch sea salt
2 tablespoons maple syrup
2 teaspoons vegan butter

Pinch sea salt
3 drops almond extract
1/4 cup natural sugar
1/2 teaspoon ground cinnamon

1. Preheat the oven to 350°F. Line a baking sheet with waxed paper or Silpat and set aside. Place nuts and a pinch of salt in one layer in a shallow baking pan and roast for 8 to 10 minutes, stirring once.

2. In a small skillet, stir together syrup, vegan butter, and salt. Simmer 2 minutes, stirring frequently. Add the toasted nuts and cook 1 minute or until syrup has mostly adhered to the nuts. Remove the pan from the heat and add the almond extract. Stir to incorporate. Pour the nuts onto the prepared baking sheet and spread them into a single layer to cool until they are cool enough to handle.

3. Combine the sugar and cinnamon in a bowl or small plastic food storage bag. Add the nuts and either roll or shake them in the mixture to coat, breaking the nuts apart as you add them. Store covered at room temperature.

sweet potato layer cake
with butterscotch-bourbon cream

Yield: 8 servings

The luscious butterscotch sauce in this recipe may seem over the top, but trust me, it's worth it. The contrasting appearances, tastes, and textures of the two butterscotch components add up to a devastatingly decadent dessert. Be sure to pass the leftover sauce, warmed, for ladling on top of each slice, because if a little is good, more is most assuredly better. **Note:** Vegan butterscotch chips can be found in natural food stores or online; the Food Lion store brand is vegan.

Butterscotch-Bourbon Cream (make the day before):
11 ounces vegan butterscotch chips
2 teaspoons bourbon
1 (12-ounce) box extra-firm silken tofu
1/4 teaspoon almond extract
1/4 teaspoon vanilla extract
Pinch sea salt
2 teaspoons lemon zest

Cake:
1 cup chopped walnuts
2 cups soy milk
4 tablespoons balsamic vinegar, divided
1 1/2 pounds sweet potatoes, peeled and grated (about 5 cups)

3 cups unbleached all-purpose flour
1/2 cup whole wheat flour, or more
1 cup light brown sugar
Pinch sea salt
2 tablespoons baking powder
2 tablespoons pumpkin pie spice
1/2 cup canola oil
1/2 teaspoon vanilla
2 teaspoons baking soda
2 tablespoons bourbon

Butterscotch Sauce:
5.5 ounces (approximately 1 cup) vegan butterscotch chips
2 tablespoons plain soy creamer

1. **Butterscotch-Bourbon Cream:** In a double boiler over medium heat, combine the butterscotch chips and bourbon and heat until the chips start to melt. Alternatively, the chips may be heated at 30 second intervals in the microwave. Whisk the melted chips vigorously until they are smooth and creamy. Cool to room temperature.

2. In a food processor, combine the tofu, butterscotch mixture, almond and vanilla extracts, and a pinch of salt. Process until smooth and creamy, scraping down the sides of the bowl as necessary. Add lemon zest and pulse to incorporate. Scrape the mixture into an airtight container and refrigerate overnight. It will thicken as it chills.

3. **Cake:** Preheat the oven to 350°F. Grease and flour two 9-inch cake pans and set aside. Spread the walnuts on a baking sheet and toast them for about 10 minutes or until golden and with a faint toasted aroma. Set aside. In a medium bowl, whisk together the soy milk and 2 tablespoons of the balsamic vinegar.

4. In a large bowl, whisk together both flours, the sugar, salt, baking powder, and

pumpkin pie spice. Whisk the canola oil and vanilla into the soy milk mixture. Make a well in the center of the dry ingredients and pour the wet ingredients into it. Stir the mixture with a wooden spoon to incorporate the wet into the dry ingredients. When partially combined, add the sweet potato and stir until all ingredients are well combined.

5. In a small bowl, whisk the remaining 2 tablespoons of vinegar with the baking soda. When it fizzes up, incorporate it well into the batter.

6. Divide the batter evenly between the prepared cake pans and gently smooth the tops. Bake for 25 to 30 minutes or until the cake pulls slightly away from the sides of the pan, a wooden pick inserted in the center comes out clean, and the top of the cake is golden brown and fairly firm. Remove the pans from the oven and allow the cakes to cool in the pans for 10 minutes. Run a knife around the sides of the cakes and invert onto a wire rack to cool.

7. Cool the cakes completely. Brush the tops of each layer with about 1 tablespoon of bourbon. If not assembling the cake immediately, wrap the layers tightly and store in the refrigerator for a day or two.

8. **Butterscotch Sauce:** In a double boiler over medium-high, heat butterscotch chips and soy creamer together until the chips start to melt. Alternatively, the chips may-be heated at 30 second intervals in the microwave. Whisk vigorously until the mixture is smooth and creamy. Allow the sauce to cool enough so that it is pourable, but not warm, or it will melt the butterscotch cream.

9. **To assemble:** Place one layer, top down, on a serving platter. Spread the top surface with half of the Butterscotch-Bourbon Cream, leaving a one-half inch margin. Sprinkle with half of the reserved walnuts and repeat layers. With a small spoon, scoop up the butterscotch sauce and drizzle it around the top edge of the cake, allowing some to cascade down the sides, and crisscross more over the top. Save some to pass, slightly reheating it if it begins to harden.

apple tart with peanut butter streusel

Yield: 8 servings

Fortunately for us, apples span both the fall and winter seasons. And perhaps no combination is better-loved than apples and peanut butter. Here, the flavors and textures of that classic snack duo are celebrated in a tempting dessert.

Tart:
1 3/4 cups all-purpose flour, divided
Pinch of sea salt
1/4 cup plus 2 tablespoons non-hydro-
    genated coconut oil (semi-solid at
    room temperature)
2/3 cup ice water
1 tablespoon canola oil
3 large sweet-tart apples (such as
    Braeburn), halved, cored, and thinly
    sliced

2 tablespoons natural sugar

Streusel:
1/2 cup all-purpose flour
1/2 cup packed brown sugar
2 tablespoons canola oil
1/3 cup plus 2 teaspoons crunchy all-natural
    peanut butter

1. *Tart:* Preheat the oven to 400°F. Combine 1 1/2 cups of the flour, salt, and coconut oil in a food processor and pulse a few times until the coconut oil is evenly distributed and the dough looks like coarse sand. Begin adding water, 2 tablespoons at a time, pulsing a few times after each, until the dough comes together. It should be slightly moist, but not sticky, and very easy to handle. Gather the dough together in a ball and break the dough into pieces over the bottom and sides of a fluted 9-inch tart pan with a removable bottom and press the pieces together, using your fingers to form the crust into a uniform thickness. Bake for 8 to 10 minutes or until slightly golden and remove from the oven. Press down any area that might have risen slightly.

2. Heat the canola oil in a large skillet over medium-high heat. Add the apples and sauté, stirring frequently, for 5 minutes. Reduce the heat if necessary to keep the apples from sticking. They should be slightly softened at the end of the cooking time and may have developed some color. Remove the pan from the heat and let the apples cool 3 to 4 minutes. Add the sugar and the remaining 1/4 cup flour and stir until well distributed. Spread the filling evenly in the crust.

3. *Streusel:* Combine the flour and sugar in a medium bowl and stir with a fork to combine. Drizzle in the oil and add the peanut butter. Mix well to combine, then crumble the streusel evenly over the top. Bake the tart for 15 minutes or longer, just until the apples are easily pierced with a sharp knife. If the crust or streusel begins to brown too quickly, cover with foil, shiny side up. When the tart is finished baking, transfer it from the oven to a wire rack and let cool for at least an hour before serving.

chocolate-orange mousse

Yield: 8 servings

This is a luscious marriage of rich chocolate and fresh oranges. Spiked with orange liqueur, it is a wonderful dessert for a cold winter evening. The mousse sets up almost instantly, so it is ready and waiting as soon as you put your dinner fork down.

2 large oranges
12 ounces extra-firm silken tofu
1/2 cup natural sugar
9 ounces bittersweet vegan chocolate, melted (see note) and slightly cooled
1 teaspoon vanilla extract

1/4 teaspoon almond extract
Pinch sea salt
Optional garnishes: Chantilly "Whipped Cream" (page 153) or other vegan whipped topping, orange slices, or candied violets

1. Arrange 8 (4-ounce) ramekins in a 9 x 13-inch pan and set aside. Zest and juice the oranges and transfer to a food processor along with the orange pulp, discarding the seeds and pith. Add the tofu and sugar to the food processor, and process until very smooth, scraping down the sides of the bowl with a rubber spatula as needed. Add the melted chocolate, vanilla and almond extracts, and a pinch of salt. Process for several minutes until smooth and fluffy, scraping down the sides of the bowl as necessary.

2. Divide the mixture evenly among the ramekins. Cover the top of the pan with foil. This method is faster than covering each individual ramekin and makes them easier to transport. Chill the mousse until set, about 30 minutes. Serve chilled, garnished as desired.

Note: Melt the chocolate in a heatproof bowl in the microwave for about a minute at 30 second intervals, whisking in between. Alternately, melt on the stove in the top of a double boiler.

ginger streusel pear pie

Yield: 8 servings

This pie crust is so flaky and delicious you almost don't need the filling. But only almost. The pear filling is set off perfectly with a fresh ginger streusel and pairs beautifully with Cinnamon Stick-Vanilla Bean Ice Cream (page 171). As an added bonus, the pie bakes in the blink of an eye because the pears are pre-cooked for a few minutes on the stovetop.

Pie Crust:
2 cups whole-wheat flour
1/2 cup non-hydrogenated coconut oil (semi-solid at room temperature)
14 tablespoons of iced water (place a few cubes of ice in a small bowl and fill with water)

Filling:
1 tablespoon canola oil
3 large ripe pears, sliced
2 tablespoons natural sugar

4 tablespoons unbleached all-purpose flour

Streusel:
1/2 cup unbleached all-purpose flour
1/2 cup whole-wheat flour
1/2 cup packed brown sugar
1/2 teaspoon ground cinnamon
Pinch nutmeg
1 tablespoon fresh grated ginger
6 tablespoons canola oil
1/2 cup coarsely chopped pecans

1. **Pie Crust:** Preheat the oven to 400°F. Combine the flour and coconut oil in a food processor and pulse a few times until the coconut oil is evenly distributed and the dough looks like coarse sand. Add water, 2 tablespoons at a time, pulsing a few times after each, until the dough comes together. It should be slightly moist, but not sticky. You may not need the full amount of water. Gather the dough together in a ball. Lightly flour your work surface and rolling pin and roll the dough out. Gently lift and transfer it into your pie pan, trimming around the rim with a sharp knife and crimping the edges. Bake 8 to 10 minutes or until slightly golden. Remove from the oven and press down any area on the crust that might have risen.

2. **Filling:** Heat the oil in a large skillet over medium-high heat. Add the pears and sauté, stirring frequently, for 5 minutes or until slightly softened. Reduce the heat if necessary to keep the pears from sticking or cooking too quickly. Remove the pan from the heat and let the pears cool 2 to 3 minutes. Stir in the sugar and flour until well distributed.

3. **Streusel:** In a medium bowl, use a fork to stir together both flours, the sugar, cinnamon, nutmeg, and ginger. Drizzle in the oil and incorporate well. Stir in the pecans. Spread the filling evenly into the crust and crumble the streusel evenly over the top. Bake for 15 minutes, or until the pears are easily pierced with a sharp knife. If the pie begins to brown too quickly, cover with foil, shiny side up. Transfer to a wire rack and let cool for at least an hour before serving.

cinnamon stick-vanilla bean ice cream

Yield: 4 to 6 servings

This ice cream is especially good served with the Ginger Streusel Pear Pie (page 170). Make the ice cream the day before you plan to serve it.

1/2 cup soy milk, divided
1 cup plain soy creamer
3/4 cup natural sugar
2 cinnamon sticks, broken in half
1 large vanilla bean pod, split lengthwise, and seeds scraped out

2 tablespoons arrowroot powder
1/2 teaspoon vanilla extract (or more
  to taste)
1 1/2 cups vegan sour cream
2 teaspoons fresh lemon juice, optional

1. Combine 1/4 cup soy milk, soy creamer, sugar, cinnamon sticks, and vanilla seeds in a 1-quart saucepan over medium heat and bring just to a boil.

2. In a small bowl, whisk the remaining 1/4 cup soy milk with the arrowroot powder until smooth. When the soy creamer mixture just reaches a boil, remove the pan from the heat and whisk in the soy milk-arrowroot mixture until smooth and thickened. Stir in the vanilla extract. Allow the custard to cool to room temperature. Whisk it again if lumps remain. Cover the custard and refrigerate it at least three hours or overnight.

3. Remove the cinnamon sticks, whisk one more time, and then whisk in the sour cream. Freeze the ice cream according to your ice cream maker's manufacturer's directions. Scrape the ice cream into an airtight container and store in the freezer. Allow the ice cream to further set up before serving if desired.

pear-rum cupcakes
with tea-infused buttercream frosting

Yield: 12 cupcakes

The only thing more satisfying than enjoying these luscious cupcakes with a cup of English Breakfast tea is savoring the same deeply earthy flavor of a cup of tea in the creamy frosting. Note: the tea for the frosting should be steeped a day ahead of time.

Cupcakes:
2 medium (4 ounce) pears, cored, and
  quartered
1/4 cup plus 2 tablespoons soy milk
1 1/4 cups unbleached all-purpose flour
1/4 cup whole wheat flour
3/4 cup natural sugar
1 tablespoon baking powder
1/2 teaspoon ground cinnamon
1/4 teaspoon ground nutmeg
1/8 teaspoon ground cloves
Pinch sea salt

1/4 cup canola oil
1/4 teaspoon vanilla
2 teaspoons rum extract
1 tablespoon apple cider vinegar
1 teaspoon baking soda

Frosting:
6 tablespoons soy creamer
3 English Breakfast tea bags
6 tablespoons vegan butter
6 tablespoons vegetable shortening
5 1/4 cups confectioners' sugar

1. **Cupcakes:** Preheat the oven to 350°F. Line a 12-cup muffin tin with muffin papers. In a food processor, pulse one pear until it is finely chopped. Transfer to a bowl and set aside. In the same food processor, process the other pear with the soy milk until smooth.

2. In a large bowl, whisk together both flours, the sugar, baking powder, cinnamon, nutmeg, cloves, and salt. Make a well in the center of the dry ingredients and pour into it the pear-soy milk mixture, oil, vanilla, and rum extract.

3. In a small bowl, stir together the vinegar and baking soda, then add to the wet ingredients in the center of the bowl. Stir just until the wet and dry ingredients are completely combined. Fold in the chopped pear. Fill the muffin cups 3/4 full with batter and bake for 22 minutes or until a wooden pick inserted in the center comes out clean. Remove the pan from the oven and let the cupcakes cool in the pan for 10 minutes, or until cool enough to handle. Remove the cupcakes from the pan and cool completely on the rack.

4. **Frosting:** In a 1-quart saucepan over medium-high heat, bring the soy creamer to a simmer. Place the tea bags in a small heatproof bowl and pour the creamer over them. Alternatively, you may heat the creamer for about 30 seconds in the microwave. Allow the tea to steep for about 3 minutes or until the bags are cool enough to handle, then gently squeeze the moisture out of the bags, being care-

ful not to tear them. Cover and chill the creamer-tea mixture over night. Whisk the mixture before using.

5. Use an electric mixer to cream the butter and shortening. Beat in 1 cup of confectioners' sugar, 1/2 cup at a time, and then beat in the tea-infused creamer. Add the remaining confectioners' sugar, 1/2 cup at a time, beating well after each addition, until the desired consistency is reached. Frost the cooled cupcakes with a generous amount of frosting. If not serving immediately, refrigerate in an air tight container.

orange-espresso chocolate chip and hazelnut cookies

Yield: 3 1/2 dozen cookies

It is difficult to top good 'ole chocolate chip cookies, but this combination of ingredients does it. The zippy citrus, roasted coffee flavor, and crunchy hazelnuts combined with the chocolate is pure cookie magic. Espresso powder can be a little challenging to find, but not to worry. Regular espresso ground to a powder in a home coffee grinder works equally well.

1/2 cup vegan butter
1/2 cup vegetable shortening
1/2 cup light brown sugar
1/2 cup natural sugar
1/4 cup soy milk
1 tablespoon orange zest
1 teaspoon vanilla
2 1/4 cups flour

1 teaspoon baking soda
1 teaspoon espresso powder or regular espresso ground to a powder in a coffee grinder
1/4 teaspoon ground cinnamon
3/4 cup vegan semi-sweet or dark chocolate chips
3/4 cup chopped hazelnuts

1. Preheat the oven to 350°F. In the large bowl of an electric mixer, cream the vegan butter, shortening, brown sugar, and sugar until light and fluffy. On the lowest speed, slowly mix in the soy milk, orange zest, and vanilla. Turn off the mixer, and add the flour, baking soda, espresso powder, and cinnamon. Mix on low speed just until well combined. Turn off the mixer and add the chocolate chips and the hazelnuts. Mix on the lowest speed until evenly incorporated, or fold in by hand.

2. Drop by two teaspoonfuls onto parchment or Silpat-lined cookie sheets (I use a small scoop), flatten slightly with your fingers, and bake for about 10 minutes or until golden brown and set. Cool slightly on cookie sheets and then remove to racks to cool completely. Store in airtight containers.

sweet and savory nut brittle

Yield: about 1 pound

This nut brittle can be enjoyed as candy or it can be crushed over salads or other savory foods. I like to make it with a variety of nuts, from almonds, cashews, and macadamia nuts, to peanuts and pecans. The balsamic vinegar and spices enhance the flavor; a little sea salt pressed into the top is the perfect finish.

1 cup natural sugar
1/4 cup water
2 tablespoons balsamic vinegar
6 tablespoons maple syrup

1 1/4 cups nuts
Optional: 2 pinches chili powder, curry
    powder, or other seasonings
Coarse sea salt

1. Oil a baking sheet, a 2-quart saucepan, and an off-set spatula.

2. Combine the sugar, water, vinegar and maple syrup in the saucepan. Stir to mix well over medium-high heat, and bring it to a simmer. Attach a candy thermometer to the side of the pan, making sure that the tip is in the mixture, but not touching the bottom of the pan. Reduce the heat to medium if the mixture is boiling too hard. Cook, not stirring, until the temperature on the thermometer reaches 360 degrees. This takes several minutes, but the temperature can rise rapidly especially near the end, so be sure to watch carefully.

3. Immediately remove the pan from the heat and quickly stir in the nuts and optional spices. Pour the molten candy onto the prepared baking sheet and smooth it evenly with an offset spatula.

4. Allow the candy to cool until it is barely warm. Sprinkle the top surface with coarse sea salt. Press it down gently onto surface with the offset spatula. If desired, sprinkle with the tiniest hint of chili powder, curry powder, or another seasoning blend or spice.

5. Cool the candy to room temperature. Break it into pieces, and store it in an airtight container, separating the layers with waxed paper.

Brunch

On the Weekend...

The dishes in this chapter are perfect for leisurely weekend mornings...but then why not serve them for dinner as well? To celebrate spring vegetables, try a Savory Bread Pudding made with tender asparagus or Baked Oatmeal with Fresh Berries. On a warm summer morning, enjoy the Antipasto Tart in Puff Pastry Crust, and for fall try the Sweet Potato Pancakes bathed in a bourbon-pecan maple syrup. When the weather turns cold, warm up with colorful Carrot Cake Pancakes or Pears Foster French Toast.

Brunch

fresh strawberry pancakes

Yield: 4 servings

A few of the ingredients in these farmstand-fresh pancakes may seem nontraditional for pancakes, but you will just have to trust me: these spectacular strawberry pancakes are healthy, beautiful, and sophisticated. I like them best served with fresh mint and Balsamic-Maple Syrup.

Pancakes:
1 1/2 cups soy milk
1 tablespoon balsamic vinegar
1/2 cup whole-wheat flour
1/2 cup self-rising flour
4 tablespoons self-rising cornmeal
2 tablespoons granulated sugar
1/2 teaspoon baking powder
1/4 teaspoon baking soda
1 cup finely diced fresh strawberries
4 fresh mint leaves, stacked, tightly rolled, and sliced thinly

2 tablespons vegan butter or vegetable oil

Balsamic-Maple Syrup:
1/2 cup finely diced fresh strawberries
1/2 cup pure maple syrup
1 1/2 to 2 teaspoons balsamic vinegar
4 fresh mint leaves, stacked, tightly rolled and thinly sliced
Freshly ground black pepper
Optional Garnishes: sprigs of fresh mint and whole fresh strawberries

1. **Pancakes:** Preheat the oven to 250°F. In a small bowl, whisk together the soy milk and balsamic vinegar. Set aside to curdle. In a medium mixing bowl, combine both flours, the cornmeal, sugar, baking powder, and baking soda. Mix well, make a well in the center, and pour in the soy milk mixture. Whisk together until well combined. Stir in diced strawberries and set aside.

2. Melt 1 tablespoon of the vegan butter in a large skillet or griddle over medium-high heat. Using a 1/4 cup measure, ladle the pancake batter onto the hot skillet, making pancakes, two at a time.

3. Cook 2 minutes on the first side until you get a nice rise, a few bubbles appear, and the edges appear set. Gently flip and cook another 2 minutes on the reverse. Add the remaining 1 tablespoon vegan butter, if needed. If pancakes are cooking too quickly, reduce the heat to medium.

4. When cooked through, transfer the pancakes to plates or a serving platter, keep warm in the oven and repeat with remaining butter and pancake batter.

5. **Balsamic-Maple Syrup:** In a saucepan, combine the strawberries, maple syrup, vinegar, mint leaves, and a few grindings of black pepper. Stir to combine and heat gently over medium heat until hot. Do not boil. Serve the pancakes hot, topped with the syrup, and garnished with mint leaves and a strawberry, if using.

baked oatmeal with fresh berries

Yield: 8 servings

Made from common ingredients, this uncommon breakfast treat is uncommonly good. Hot out of the oven, its texture is similar to bread pudding, and its aroma fills the house. Where I live, strawberries are in season in late spring, but you can use any of your favorite seasonal berries.

6 ounces firm silken tofu
1 cup soy milk
1/2 cup canola oil
3/4 cup natural sugar
1 tablespoon baking powder
1/2 teaspoon sea salt

3 cups old-fashioned oatmeal
2 tablespoons natural sugar
1/2 teaspoon ground cinnamon
1/2 pint of fresh berries, rinsed, drained
    and patted dry

1. Lightly grease a 9-inch glass or ceramic pie pan and set aside. Combine the tofu, soy milk, canola oil, sugar, baking powder, and salt in a food processor. Process until smooth, scraping down the sides of the bowl as necessary. Transfer the mixture to a medium mixing bowl and stir in the oatmeal. Spoon this mixture into the prepared pan, gently smoothing the top. Sprinkle the surface with the remaining sugar and cinnamon, cover with foil, and refrigerate overnight.

2. When ready to bake, remove the dish from the refrigerator and preheat the oven to 350°F. Stud the top surface of the oatmeal with berries, and bake for 35 minutes or until just firm. Serve hot.

Note: The oatmeal may be reheated by covering the baking dish with foil and placing it in a cold oven. Turn the oven temperature to 300°F. and heat for about 20 minutes, or until warm.

savory bread pudding

Yield: 6 to 8 servings

Tender pieces of asparagus, red bell pepper, and mushrooms add color, texture, and flavor to this savory bread pudding that is an ideal make-ahead brunch dish.

8 ounces whole grain bread (or a baguette), torn into 1-inch pieces
1 tablespoon olive oil
1 small onion, diced
2 large garlic cloves, thinly sliced
1 medium red bell pepper, diced
8 ounces mushrooms, sliced
8 ounces thin asparagus, cut into 1-inch pieces
Sea salt and freshly ground black pepper

12 ounces firm silken tofu
1/2 cup unsweetened soy milk
2 cups vegetable stock
1/8 teaspoon dry mustard
1/8 teaspoon nutmeg
1 teaspoon vegan Worcestershire sauce or Bragg Liquid Aminos
2 tablespoons nutritional yeast, optional
2 teaspoons lemon zest

1. Preheat the oven to 350°F. Oil a 9-inch glass or ceramic pie dish. Arrange the bread on a baking sheet and bake for 8 to 10 minutes to dry it out, but not to brown it. Transfer the bread to a large mixing bowl. Leave the oven on.

2. Heat the oil in a large skillet over medium-high heat. Add the onion and garlic and sauté for 2 minutes. Add the bell pepper, mushrooms, and the asparagus and sauté for 2 minutes after each addition. Season to taste with salt and pepper. Remove the skillet from the heat.

3. In a food processor, combine the tofu, soy milk, vegetable stock, dry mustard, nutmeg, Worcestershire Sauce, nutritional yeast, if using, and salt and pepper to taste. Process until creamy and well combined, scraping down the bowl as necessary.

4. Pour the custard over the bread and toss until the mixture is well combined. Fold in the vegetables and any juice and mix until well distributed. Fold in the lemon zest. Let the mixture sit for about 10 minutes, folding ingredients together, being sure to scrape up custard from the bottom, every few minutes. Transfer the mixture to the prepared pie dish, gently smoothing the top, but not packing the ingredients down. Bake for 30 minutes or until firm, but not dried out. Serve hot or warm.

curried red-lentil "cheesecake" with tamarind sauce

Yield: 6 to 8 servings

I was first introduced to savory cheesecakes in the 1980s by my friend, caterer Monica Holmes. This luscious dish makes a wonderfully adaptable addition to the more standard brunch fare. As an alternative to the tamarind sauce, the Lemon Fig Dipping Sauce (page 26) is also delicious with this cheesecake. A crisp green salad is an ideal accompaniment.

Crust:
1 cup dry breadcrumbs
1/4 teaspoon ground coriander
Pinch sea salt
2 tablespoons olive oil, or more

Filling:
12 ounces extra-firm tofu, drained
12 ounces extra-firm silken tofu
1 tablespoon lemon juice
Sea salt
1/2 teaspoon vegan Worcestershire
    sauce, optional
1 1/2 teaspoons curry powder
1 teaspoon garam masala
1/2 teaspoon ground cumin
1/4 teaspoon dry mustard
1/4 teaspoon ground ginger
1/4 teaspoon turmeric
3/4 cup red lentils
1 1/2 cups water

1 tablespoon olive oil
1 small yellow onion, chopped
Freshly ground black pepper
3 garlic cloves, minced
1 large orange bell pepper, chopped
4 ounces fresh stemmed spinach, coarsely
    chopped

Sauce:
1 1/2 cups water, divided
4 ounces tamarind pulp, torn into 1-inch
    pieces
2 teaspoons mild molasses
1/8 teaspoon ground cumin
1/8 teaspoon ground ginger
1/8 teaspoon garam masala
1/8 teaspoon garlic powder
1/8 teaspoon onion powder
1/2 teaspoon natural sugar, or more
Garnish: chopped cashews

1. *Crust:* Preheat the oven to 350°F. In a small bowl, combine the breadcrumbs, coriander, and salt. Add the olive oil, one tablespoon at a time, mixing until crumbs hold together, adding more oil if needed. Gently press the crust into the bottom of an 8-inch springform pan. Bake 8 to 10 minutes or until the crust is golden. Set aside on a wire rack.

2. *Filling:* Combine both tofus, lemon juice, a pinch of salt, Worcestershire sauce, if using, curry powder, garam masala, cumin, dry mustard, ginger, and turmeric in a food processor. Process until smooth, scraping down the sides as necessary. Set aside.

3. In a 1-quart saucepan over medium-high heat, bring water and a pinch of salt to a gentle boil. Stir in lentils and simmer, uncovered, for 10 minutes or until lentils are

soft and the water has evaporated. Stir frequently so that the lentils do not stick. Remove the pan from the heat.

4. Heat the oil in a large skillet over medium high heat. Add the onion and sauté until it begins to soften. Add a pinch of salt, freshly ground black pepper, and garlic, and continue to sauté for 1 minute or until the garlic softens and turns golden, making sure not to allow it to scorch. Add the bell pepper and spinach and cook until the spinch is wilted. Remove the pan from the heat. Stir in the cooked lentils, combining well.

5. Fold the creamed tofu into the lentil and vegetable mixture until well combined. Check for seasoning and adjust if desired. Spoon the batter evenly into the crust, gently smoothing the top, and return the pan to the oven for 45 minutes or until the cheesecake develops a little color on top and is almost firm. Turn off the oven and let the cheesecake sit for an additional 5 minutes. Transfer to a wire rack and let it cool for 10 to 15 minutes.

6. *Sauce:* In a 1-quart saucepan, bring 1 cup of water to a boil. Add the tamarind and simmer for 5 minutes or until it begins to break down. Press it through a strainer into a medium bowl, pressing hard on the solids to force a creamy pulp through the strainer. Discard the fibrous solids. Return the pulp to the saucepan and slowly whisk in 1/2 cup water. Whisk in all remaining ingredients except cashews. Bring to a simmer, stirring constantly, and cook until hot. Check for tartness and add the sugar, 1/2 teaspoon at a time, until you achieve the desired balance of flavors. Remove the pan from the heat.

7. *To serve:* Run a knife carefully around the edge of the pan and remove the sides. Serve the cheesecake warm or room temperature topped with warm sauce and chopped cashews.

antipasto tart in puff pastry crust

Yield: 4 servings

This dish was born out of a desire for a balanced meal starring fresh raw tomatoes. The filling is a mélange of fresh tomatoes, white beans, and Mediterranean flavors. A tahini dressing lightly binds the ingredients together. This meal is pretty enough for company, yet simple enough for a weeknight family dinner.

1 box Pepperidge Farm puff pastry, thawed
2 tablespoons tahini (sesame paste)
2 tablespoons fresh lemon juice
1/2 teaspoon maple syrup
1/4 teaspoon olive oil
1 1/2 teaspoons fresh sage, minced (or 1/2 teaspoon dry rubbed)
Sea salt and freshly ground black pepper
2 cups diced tomato (2 medium tomatoes)

1/2 cup diced marinated artichoke hearts, well drained
1/2 cup diced marinated mushrooms
1/4 cup chopped, cooked cippoline onions or scallions
4 roasted garlic cloves, chopped
1/4 cup lightly packed coarsely chopped fresh basil
1 (15-ounce) can cannellini beans, rinsed and drained
Garnish: 4 sprigs fresh basil

1. Preheat the oven to 400°F. Line two baking sheets with Silpat or spray the sheets lightly with non-stick spray. Unfold one sheet of puff pastry on each sheet, pressing it together at the seams if necessary.

2. Lightly flour a rolling pin and roll the dough out slightly to accommodate two 6-inch circles on each sheet. Arrange a 6-inch saucer upside down on the first sheet and cut around it with a sharp paring knife. Repeat on the same sheet to make a second crust. Repeat with the second sheet of pastry.

3. On each circle, score a line about 1/2-inch inside the outside edge with the tip of your knife; avoid cutting all the way through. When the crusts bake, this will form a rim. With fork tines, liberally prick the surface of the dough inside the scored line (not the rim). Bake the crusts for 15 minutes or until golden brown. Remove the baking sheet from the oven and, with a spoon, gently press or crush down the center of each crust, which will have puffed, stopping at the rim. Slide the shells onto plates.

4. In a bowl, whisk together the tahini, lemon juice, maple syrup, olive oil, sage, salt, and pepper. Set aside. In a medium bowl, combine the tomato, artichoke, mushrooms, onions, garlic, basil, and beans. Toss gently with the tahini mixture until well incorporated. Use a slotted spoon to fill each shell with one-quarter of the antipasto mixture. Garnish and serve slightly warm or at room temperature.

banana-blueberry sour-cream coffee cake

Yield: 12 servings

This moist coffee cake was inspired by blueberry picking at our friends' farm on Virginia's Eastern Shore during berry season. Fresh raspberries or blackberries may be used instead or in combination.

Cake:
1/2 cup vegan butter, softened
1 cup light brown sugar, packed
1 banana, quartered
2 cups self-rising flour
1 cup vegan sour cream
2 teaspoons lemon zest
3 cups blueberries, divided

Streusel Topping:
1/4 cup melted or softened vegan butter

1/2 cup brown sugar
1/2 cup unbleached all-purpose flour
1/2 cup old fashioned or quick cooking oatmeal
1 teaspoon pumpkin pie spice (or 3/4 teaspoon cinnamon + 1/4 teaspoon nutmeg)
1/2 cup pecans or walnuts

1. *Cake:* Preheat oven to 375°F. Spray a 9 x 13-inch baking pan with non-stick cooking spray and set aside.

2. In a large mixing bowl, cream together the butter and sugar on high speed of an electric mixer fitted with a paddle attachment. Beat in the banana until combined. Add the flour and sour cream, and blend on low speed until completely incorporated. Avoid overbeating. Gently stir in 2 cups of berries by hand. Spoon the batter into the prepared pan and spread evenly. Sprinkle the remaining cup of berries evenly over the top.

3. *Streusel Topping:* In a medium bowl, combine all the ingredients and mix until crumbly. Sprinkle the streusel on top of the cake.

4. *To bake:* Bake for about 40 minutes or until the center springs back when gently pressed with fingers. It is a little difficult to tell when this cake is done, as the traditional wooden pick tester method is deceiving because the berries are so juicy and the pick always comes out moist. So, trust your oven, your fingers, and your eyes. Cool the coffee cake for 15 minutes before serving. Store tightly covered in refrigerator.

fresh fruit and "cream cheese" pastry pinwheels

Yield: 4 servings

Summer brings us an abundance of fresh fruits, from apricots, peaches, and nectarines, to an assortment of berries. Choose your favorite fruits for these yummy pinwheels made with flaky puff pastry and a creamy filling. Because the fruit and "cream cheese" fillings need time to cool, I recommend making them the night before you plan to serve the pinwheels so they can be assembled quickly in the morning. To save time, you can use storebought vegan cream cheese instead of the homemade cream cheese filling in the recipe.

Fruit Filling:
1 cup chopped fresh apricots, peaches,
   or nectarines
1/2 cup fresh blueberries
1 tablespoon brandy or fresh lemon
   juice
2 tablespoons natural sugar

"Cream Cheese" Filling:
6 ounces firm silken tofu

1/4 cup white granulated sugar
1 tablespoon fresh lemon juice
2 1/2 tablespoons unbleached all-purpose
   flour
1/4 teaspoon vanilla extract
1/8 teaspoon almond extract

Pastry:
1 box Pepperidge Farm Puff Pastry, thawed
Confectioners' sugar for dusting, optional

1. *Fruit Filling:* Combine the fruit, brandy, and sugar in a medium saucepan over medium heat. Stir the mixture well and simmer, stirring with a wooden spoon, until the fruit begins to break down and the mixture thickens, about 4 minutes. Really juicy fruits like strawberries will appear to produce so much juice that they will never thicken, but the juice will cook off after about 8 minutes. Cool to room temperature and set aside if using right away or cover and refrigerate it until ready to use.

2. *"Cream Cheese" filling:* Combine the tofu, sugar, lemon juice, flour, vanilla, and almond extract in a food processor. Process until smooth, scraping down the sides of the bowl as necessary. Refrigerate the mixture at least an hour to chill.

3. *Pastry:* Preheat the oven to 400°F. Position two racks near the middle of the oven. Line two baking sheets with parchment paper or Silpat and set aside. Working with one sheet of pastry at a time, unfold it on a work surface. Pinch together and smooth the creases if necessary. With a sharp knife, slice the sheet of pastry vertically and horizontally in half to make four squares. Make a diagonal cut from all four corners of each square to within a generous inch of their centers.

4. Carefully transfer the four squares to a baking sheet, placing them several inches apart and trying not to distort their shapes. Repeat with the remaining sheet of pastry. Place a generous tablespoon of cream cheese in the center of each square.

5. Form each square into a pinwheel by folding every other point up to the center and pressing gently. The four alternating folded points should meet in the center. Place a generous tablespoon of fruit filling in the center of each pinwheel where the points come together. Slightly flatten the mound of fruit.

6. Bake for 15 minutes or until puffed and golden. Remove the pans from the oven and cool for 1 to 2 minutes. With a spatula, slide each pinwheel onto a serving platter or individual plates. Serve warm with a dusting of confectioners' sugar, if using.

blueberry and lemon verbena pancakes

Yield: 4 servings

Lemon verbena is a beautiful green herb that grows easily in fragrant bushes and comes back year after year. If you don't grow lemon verbena, you should, if for no other reason than to enjoy these pancakes.

1/2 cup whole wheat flour
1/2 cup self-rising flour
32 lemon verbena leaves, rinsed, drained, and dried inside a dish towel
4 tablespoons natural sugar
1/2 teaspoon baking powder
1/4 teaspoon baking soda

1 1/2 cups soy milk
1 cup fresh blueberries, rinsed and drained
Vegan butter
Canola oil
Maple Syrup
Garnish: fresh blueberries and fresh sprigs of lemon verbena

1. Preheat the oven to 250°F. In a food processor, combine both flours and lemon verbena leaves. Pulse until you see tiny flecks of the green leaves dispersed through the flour. Transfer the flour mixture into a medium mixing bowl and combine with the sugar, baking powder, and baking soda. Make a well in the center of the dry ingredients and pour in the soy milk. Whisk both together until well combined. Stir in the blueberries.

2. In a large skillet or griddle over medium-high heat, melt together 1/2 tablespoon each of the vegan butter and oil. Using a 1/4 cup measure, make pancakes, two at a time. Cook 2 to 3 minutes on the first side until you get a nice rise, a few bubbles appear, and the edges appear set. Gently flip the pancakes and cook another 2 minutes.

3. Add butter and oil to keep the skillet greased as needed. If the pancakes are cooking too quickly, lower heat to medium. When they are cooked through, remove the pancakes to plates or a serving platter, and keep warm. Repeat with additional butter, oil, and remaining pancake batter. Serve each stack with a drizzle of maple syrup, a few blueberries and a sprig of lemon verbena.

herb biscuits
with southern-style tomato-basil gravy

Yield: 6 servings

Inspired by my Southern childhood, I created this light, fresh Tomato-Basil Gravy using Liquid Smoke and tomatoes off the vine. I serve it with the flakiest biscuits imaginable, and your favorite tempeh bacon makes a perfect side dish. Be sure to freeze the shortening and butter ahead of time.

1 tablespoon apple cider vinegar
1 cup unsweetened soy milk
2 cups self-rising flour
2 tablespoons minced fresh rosemary

4 tablespoons frozen vegetable shortening
2 tablespoons soft vegan butter plus 4 tablespoons frozen
Southern Style Tomato-Basil Gravy (recipe follows)

1. Preheat the oven to 425°F. In a small bowl, whisk the vinegar into the soy milk and set aside. In a large bowl, combine the flour and rosemary and stir with a fork to combine. Make a well in the center. Grate the frozen shortening and butter into the well. Whisk the soy milk mixture and add it to the well.

2. Incorporate the wet into the dry ingredients by stirring with a fork. Place the remaining 2 tablespoons of butter in a 9-inch square pan and place it in the oven to melt the butter. Remove the pan as soon as the butter has melted.

3. On a lightly floured work surface, pat or roll the dough to 3/4-inch thick. Fold it like a business letter: fold one side two-thirds of the way across and fold the remaining 1/3 back across. Pat or gently roll the dough out to a 3/4-inch thickness again, turn it a quarter turn and repeat about 4 more times.

4. Lightly flour the work surface as necessary. The last time you pat the dough to 3/4-inch, cut out biscuits with a 2-inch biscuit or cookie-cutter, or a drinking glass. Place each biscuit in the prepared pan and flip to coat both sides with melted butter. Bake the biscuits for about 15 minutes or until golden brown. Serve open-faced, topped with the gravy.

southern-style tomato-basil gravy

Yield: about 2 1/2 cups

1 tablespoon canola oil
1 small red onion, chopped
2 garlic cloves, minced
3/4 teaspoon Liquid Smoke (or to taste)
Pinch sea salt
4 large Roma tomatoes, cut into 1/3-
   inch dice

6 large basil leaves, stacked, rolled tightly,
   and thinly sliced
1 cup unsweetened soy milk
1 tablespoon unbleached all-purpose flour
1 tablespoon cool water
1 tablespoon fresh lemon juice
Sea salt and freshly ground black pepper

1. Heat the oil in a large skillet over medium-high heat. Add the onion, and sauté for about 3 minutes or until it softens. Add the garlic and a pinch of salt and continue to sauté for about 2 minutes or until both the onion and the garlic begin to caramelize. Reduce heat if necessary. Add Liquid Smoke and sauté for another minute.

2. Add the tomatoes and cook for 3 to 5 minutes or until the tomatoes soften, but still hold their shape. Add basil and soy milk. Cook, stirring well, for 1 to 2 minutes to heat through. Whisk together flour and water and stir into the tomato mixture. Cook for another 2 to 3 minutes or until the flour no longer tastes raw. After 1 to 2 minutes of cooking, stir in the lemon juice, and salt and pepper to taste. Check for seasoning and adjust if necessary.

rice cakes
with plum and sake-maple syrup

Yield: 4 servings

Some leftover brown rice and the gift of beautiful ruby-red fresh plums from a friend's tree gave rise to this pancake recipe. You will swoon for the crisp buttery crust on the rice cakes complemented by the flavorful syrup. For a lovely garnish, consider topping each serving with a spoonful of sweetened vegan sour cream with a hint of vanilla and sprigs of fresh mint.

Plum and Sake-Maple Syrup:
2 cups sake
1 cup maple syrup
1 cup chopped pitted ripe plums

Rice Cakes:
2 cups cooked brown rice, cooled
1/2 cup whole wheat flour

1/2 cup self-rising flour
2 tablespoons natural sugar
1 teaspoon baking powder
1/2 teaspoon baking soda
1 1/2 cups soy milk, or more
Vegan butter
Canola oil

1. **Plum and Sake-Maple Syrup:** Combine the sake and maple syrup in a saucepan over medium-high heat and heat to simmering. Add the plums and simmer until heated through. Transfer the plums to a bowl and cover to keep warm. Continue simmering the sake-syrup mixture until slightly thickened and reduced. Return the plums to the syrup and heat until hot. The syrup is now ready to use.

2. **Rice Cakes:** Preheat the oven to 250°F. In a medium mixing bowl, combine the brown rice, both flours, sugar, baking powder, and baking soda. Make a well in the center and pour in the soy milk. Whisk together the wet and dry ingredients with a fork until well combined. The batter will be fairly thick and hold its shape. If the batter is too dry, add up to 1/2 cup more soy milk, a little at a time.

3. In a large skillet or griddle over medium-high heat, melt together 1/2 tablespoon of the vegan butter and the oil. Using a scant 1/4 cup measure, make pancakes, two at a time. Cook 2 to 3 minutes on the first side until you get a slight rise, a few bubbles appear, and the edges appear set. Gently flip the pancakes and cook another 2 minutes. Add butter and oil to keep the skillet greased as needed. If the pancakes are cooking too quickly, reduce the heat to medium.

4. Transfer the cooked pancakes to plates or a serving platter and keep them warm in the oven. Repeat with additional butter, oil and remaining pancake batter.

5. **To serve:** Arrange two pancakes on each of four plates and top with the syrup.

cranberry, walnut, and "blue cheese" tartlets

Yield: 4 servings

I make this festive-but-simple fall brunch dish in the shape of hearts, but simple circles or diamonds would be lovely too. The combination of ingredients is just made for baking up in these little puffs of goodness. These are perfect for Thanksgiving morning or as part of an hors d'oeuvre buffet.

1 tablespoon walnut oil
1/2 cup chopped onion
1/2 cup fresh cranberries
1/2 cup coarsely chopped walnuts
1 tablespoon natural sugar
1 teaspoon fresh thyme leaves, plus
    more for garnish

1/2 teaspoon balsamic vinegar
Sea salt and freshly ground black pepper
1 sheet Pepperidge Farm Puff Pastry,
    thawed
2 tablespoons "Blue Cheese" Sauce, plus
    more for garnish (page 92)

1. Preheat the oven to 400°F. Heat the oil in a large skillet over medium-high heat.

2. Add the onion and sauté for 3 minutes or until the onion begins to soften. Add the cranberries and sauté another 2 minutes or until they pop. Add the walnuts and sauté the mixture for 2 more minutes or until the onion is slightly golden. Stir in the sugar, thyme, balsamic vinegar, and salt and pepper to taste. Sauté 1 minute and remove the pan from the heat.

3. Transfer the mixture to a small bowl and allow it to cool while you cut out the pastry. Arrange the sheet of pastry directly on a baking sheet. I like to line the sheet with Silpat for extra non-stick assurance. With a 2 1/2-inch heart-shaped (or other shape) cookie cutter, cut out 8 hearts or other shapes. Lift off the pastry sheet leaving the hearts in place on the baking sheet. Be sure they are separated as much as possible.

4. Stir the 2 tablespoons blue cheese sauce into the cranberry mixture and place about 2 rounded teaspoons of filling in the center of each heart. Press the filling down lightly in the center to flatten. Bake 16 to 17 minutes or until golden brown. The pastry will puff around the filling. Remove the baking sheet from the oven to a wire rack and transfer the pastries, as soon as they are cool enough to handle, to a serving platter or plates. Garnish each with a tiny dab of blue cheese sauce and a sprinkling of fresh thyme leaves. Serve hot or warm.

migas with green tomato-chili sauce

Yield: 4 servings

Migas is traditionally a Tex-Mex scramble of eggs, tortillas, cheese, spices, and fresh vegetables topped with a zesty sauce. My version is an addicting combination of tofu, sautéed tortillas, and a host of bright flavors. I love this dish so much, I could eat it morning, noon, or night. Topped with my Green Tomato-Chili Sauce, this recipe is a great way to use fresh green tomatoes, although you can top the migas with your favorite salsa if you don't have time to make the green tomato-chile sauce.

2 tablespoons canola oil, divided
1 small yellow onion, chopped
1/2 orange bell pepper, chopped
Sea salt and freshly ground black pepper
2 cloves garlic minced
4 corn tortillas, torn into bite size pieces
1/2 teaspoon ground cumin
1/2 teaspoon ground coriander
1/2 teaspoon ground chipotle powder

2 tablespoons nutritional yeast, divided
14 ounces extra-firm tofu, pressed and drained
4 tablespoons minced cilantro
4 tablespoons vegan sour cream
2 Roma tomatoes, cut into 1/4-inch dice
1/4 cup toasted pumpkin seeds
Green tomato-chili sauce (recipe follows)
4 lime wedges and 4 cilantro sprigs for garnish

1. Heat 1 tablespoon of the canola oil in a large skillet over medium-high heat. Add the onion, bell pepper and a pinch of salt, and sauté until softened, 5 minutes. Add the garlic and sauté until it turns golden and the onion becomes translucent. Move the vegetables over to the side of the skillet with your spoon and add the remaining 1 tablespoon canola oil. Add the tortillas to the oil and stir to coat, then stir to combine with the vegetables and sauté 1 to 2 minutes or until the tortillas soften and turn golden.

2. In a medium bowl, break up the tofu into irregular bite-size pieces. Add the cumin, coriander, chipotle powder, and 1 tablespoon of the nutritional yeast, and mix well to combine. Add the tofu mixture to the skillet and gently scramble for 10 minutes, stirring occasionally to scrape up browned bits from the bottom of the skillet. Reduce the heat and add a small amount of water if the migas begin to stick. Add the remaining tablespoon of nutritional yeast and continue cooking for 5 more minutes. Check the seasoning. Remove the skillet from the heat.

3. *To serve:* Transfer to a serving platter or individual plates. Spoon the green tomato chili sauce over the migas and pass any extra. Sprinkle the minced cilantro over the sauce, add dollops of sour cream, and sprinkle with diced tomatoes and pumpkin seeds. Garnish with lime wedges and cilantro sprigs.

green tomato-chili sauce

Yield: about 1 1/2 cups

This flavorful sauce makes an especially delicious topping for the migas.

2 large green tomatoes, quartered
2 (2-inch) jalapeños, seeds removed
1/2 cup vegetable stock
1 tablespoon canola oil
1/3 cup chopped yellow or orange bell
   pepper
1/3 cup chopped red onion
2 large gloves garlic, minced

2 teaspoons ground coriander
1/8 teaspoon ground cumin
1/8 teaspoon chipotle powder
Pinch natural sugar
Sea salt
1 tablespoon all-purpose flour
3 tablespoons water

1. In a food processor, combine the tomatoes, jalapeños, and vegetable stock. Process until smooth and set aside.

2. Heat the oil in a large skillet over medium-high heat. Add the onion and bell pepper, and cook for 2 minutes to soften. Add the garlic and continue to cook, stirring, until the garlic softens and the onion becomes translucent, about 3 minutes. Add the coriander, cumin, chipotle powder, sugar and salt to taste. Stir well.

3. Sprinkle with flour, followed by 3 tablespoons of water. Stir well again. Add the tomato-chili puree, stir again, and simmer for about 20 minutes to allow all flavors to marry. Stir frequently and reduce heat if necessary to prevent sauce from sticking. Remove the pan from the heat and set aside until ready to serve.

pumpkin coffee cake
with cranberry-walnut streusel

Yield: 12 servings

This is the moistest cake you may ever eat. And it becomes even more so as it sits (well-covered of course). It was inspired by a recipe I saw for a dried cranberry-nut pumpkin cake that included dried cranberries and nuts in the batter. Since I wanted to make a cake with all the flavors of autumn – but that didn't require frosting – I decided to use the dried fruit and nuts in a streusel topping instead.

Cake:
2 1/2 cups unbleached all-purpose flour
2 cups natural sugar
1 teaspoon baking powder
1 teaspoon baking soda
1 teaspoon pumpkin pie spice, or to
   taste
1/2 teaspoon salt
1(15-ounce) can solid pack pumpkin
   (or fresh pumpkin, see note)
2/3 cup walnut oil

2 to 3 tablespoons vegan sour cream
1/2 cup soy milk
2 teaspoons vanilla extract

Streusel:
1/2 cup vegan butter, room temperature
1/2 cup light brown sugar
1 teaspoon pumpkin pie spice, or more to
   taste
1 cup self-rising flour
1/2 cup dried cranberries
1/2 cup finely chopped walnuts

1. *Cake:* Preheat the oven to 350°F. Grease and flour a 9 x 13-inch baking pan and set aside. In a large bowl, whisk together the flour, sugar, baking powder, baking soda, pumpkin pie spice, and salt until well combined. Make a well in the center. In a separate medium bowl, whisk together the pumpkin, oil, sour cream, soy milk, and vanilla. Stir to completely incorporate the wet into the dry ingredients. Avoid over-mixing. Transfer the batter to the prepared pan, spreading evenly.

2. *Streusel:* In a medium bowl, crumble together the vegan butter, brown sugar, pumpkin pie spice, and flour until the clumps are fairly uniform. Add the dried cranberries and walnuts and continue to mix until all of the ingredients are well distributed.

3. *To assemble:* Crumble the streusel evenly over the top surface of the cake. Bake for 30 minutes or until a toothpick inserted into the center of the cake comes out clean. Cool the cake completely on a wire rack. Store any leftovers tightly covered.

Note: If using fresh pumpkin, you will need a generous 1 3/4 cups of homemade cooked pumpkin puree. Drain it in a coffee filter-lined sieve placed over a deep bowl for 1 to 2 hours stirring occasionally.

sweet potato pancakes with southern syrup

Yield: 4 servings

For these pancakes, I grated the sweet potato in my food processor with the grater attachment. Leaving the skin on, I was rewarded with beautiful shreds that I stirred into my go-to pancake batter along with some cool weather spices. The only thing my breakfast needed was a Southern-style Bourbon-Pecan Maple Syrup.

Pancakes:
3/4 cup self-rising flour
3/4 cup whole-wheat flour
1/4 cup light brown sugar
1/2 teaspoon baking powder
1/4 teaspoon baking soda
1 1/2 teaspoons pumpkin pie spice (or your own blend of cinnamon, nutmeg, cloves, etc.)

1 1/2 cups soy milk
2 cups lightly-packed grated sweet potato
Vegan butter
Canola oil

Southern Syrup:
1 tablespoon vegan butter
1/3 cup pecan pieces
1/2 cup maple syrup
2 teaspoons bourbon

1. *Pancakes:* Preheat the oven to 250°F. In a medium mixing bowl, combine both flours, sugar, baking powder, baking soda, and pumpkin pie spice. Make a well in the center of the dry ingredients and pour in the soy milk. Stir the ingredients together with a fork until well combined.

2. Gently stir in the grated sweet potato until completely incorporated. In a large skillet, heat 1/2 tablespoon each of the butter and the oil. Using a 1/4 cup measure, make the pancakes, two at a time. Cook a couple of minutes on the first side until you see a few bubbles, get a nice rise and the edges appear set. Gently flip the pancakes and cook another 2 to 3 minutes. Add butter and oil to the skillet to keep it greased as needed. If the pancakes are cooking too quickly, reduce the heat to medium. When the pancakes are cooked through, remove them to plates or a serving platter, and keep them warm in the preheated oven. Repeat with additional butter and oil and remaining pancake batter.

3. *Southern Syrup:* Melt the butter in a small skillet over medium-high heat. Add the pecans and sauté for 2 minutes. Reduce heat if the butter is bubbling too fast. Add the maple syrup and cook 2 minutes longer. Turn off the heat, stir in bourbon, and serve immediately over the hot pancakes.

farmstand fruit muffins

Yield: 12 muffins

Fresh picked autumn apples are especially good in these muffins. But you can enjoy them any time by substituting whatever fruit is in season. Any type of chopped nuts may be used in place of the walnuts as well.

Streusel:
4 tablespoons unbleached all-purpose
    flour
4 tablespoons natural sugar
4 tablespoons old fashioned oatmeal
4 tablespoons chopped walnuts
2 tablespoons canola oil
Pinch ground cinnamon

Muffins:
1 cup soy milk
2 teaspoons apple cider vinegar

1 cup unbleached all-purpose flour
1 cup whole wheat flour
1/2 cup natural sugar, or more for a
    sweeter version
1 tablespoon baking powder
1 teaspoon baking soda
1/2 teaspoon sea salt
Dash ground cinnamon, optional
1 cup canola oil
1 large apple, chopped (1 cup)

1. *Streusel:* Combine all the ingredients in a small bowl. Mix until moist and crumbly and set aside.

2. *Muffins:* Preheat the oven to 450°F. Line a muffin tin with 12 paper cupcake liners. Set aside.

3. In a small bowl, whisk together the soy milk and vinegar and set aside. It will curdle slightly, so whisk it a couple of times, including just before using.

4. In a large bowl, whisk together both flours, sugar, baking powder, baking soda, salt, and optional ground spice. Make a well in the center of the dry ingredients and pour in the canola oil and the soymilk mixture. Using a fork, stir together the ingredients until combined. Gently fold in the fruit. Divide the batter evenly among the muffin cups. Divide streusel evenly among muffins, sprinkling it on top, and pressing gently.

5. Bake the muffins for 20 minutes or until a wooden pick inserted into the center of one comes out clean. Remove the pan from the oven to a wire rack until the muffins are cool enough to handle. Carefully remove the muffins in their liners from the tin. Serve slightly warm or at room temperature. Store any leftovers in an airtight container in the refrigerator.

carrot cake pancakes

Yield: 4 servings

These pancakes are a delectable way to start the day. The topping is a cream cheese-orange sauce reminiscent of the vegan cream cheese frosting I'm crazy for. Consider garnishing with fresh mint sprigs, a few walnut pieces, or a sprinkling of orange zest.

Pancakes:
1/2 cup whole-wheat flour
1/2 cup self-rising flour
1/2 teaspoon baking powder
1/4 teaspoon baking soda
2 tablespoons light brown sugar
2 teaspoons pumpkin pie spice
1/2 cup soy milk
3/4 cup pineapple juice
3/4 cup finely grated carrot
1/2 cup finely chopped walnuts

1/2 teaspoon vanilla extract
Vegan butter
Canola oil

Sauce:
3/4 cup orange juice
1 tablespoon plus 1 teaspoon arrowroot powder
2 tablespoons natural sugar
1/4 cup plus 2 tablespoons vegan cream cheese
2 teaspoons lemon or orange zest

1. *Pancakes:* Preheat the oven to 250°F. In a medium mixing bowl, combine the whole-wheat flour, self-rising flour, baking powder, baking soda, sugar, and pumpkin pie spice. Make a well in the center, and add the soy milk and juice. Whisk the mixture together until it is almost combined. Add the carrots, nuts, and vanilla and whisk until well combined.

2. In a large skillet over medium-high heat, melt together 1/2 tablespoon each of the butter and canola oil. Using 1/4 cup of batter per pancake, ladle the batter to make two pancakes at a time. Cook for 2 to 3 minutes on the first side. A few bubbles will appear in the surface indicating doneness. Gently flip the pancakes and cook another 2 minutes. Transfer the cooked pancakes to a heatproof platter and place in the oven to keep warm. Continue making pancakes with the remaining pancake batter, adding additional butter and oil to the skillet to keep it greased as needed.

3. *Sauce:* In a small bowl, whisk 2 tablespoons of orange juice with the arrowroot powder until incorporated. In a small saucepan over medium-high heat, bring remaining orange juice and sugar to a gentle boil. Remove from heat and whisk in cream cheese followed by arrowroot mixture, whisking until smooth. Whisk in the zest.

4. *To assemble:* Serve the pancakes topped with the sauce. Serve immediately.

grits and greens with mushroom gravy

Yield: 6 to 8 servings

This dressed-up version of an old Southern classic is simple to prepare and just as stick-to-your ribs satisfying as its heavier forebear. If regular stone-ground grits are unavailable, you can substitute quick-cooking or instant grits in a pinch. Just prepare according to package directions, then stir in the garlic and onion powders, Worcestershire Sauce, and nutritional yeast.

Grits:
4 cups water
2 tablespoons vegan butter
1 cup stone-ground grits
3 cups unsweetened soy milk
Salt and freshly ground black pepper
1/4 teaspoon garlic powder
1/4 teaspoon onion powder
1 tablespoon of vegan Worcestershire sauce or Bragg Liquid Aminos
1/4 cup nutritional yeast flakes

Greens:
1 to 2 tablespoons olive oil
2 heads fresh kale, stemmed and chopped
1/2 teaspoon salt
1/2 cup water
3 tablespoons apple cider vinegar

2 tablespoons maple syrup
1 tablespoon chopped smoked almonds, optional

Gravy:
1 tablespoon olive oil
1/4 cup chopped onion
8 ounces mushrooms, sliced
1 tablespoon minced fresh rosemary leaves
1 (15.5-ounce) can white beans, rinsed and drained
3/4 cup water
3/4 cup vegetable stock
2 large cloves garlic
1 tablespoon dry sherry
1 teaspoon fresh lemon juice
Pinch freshly ground nutmeg
Sea salt and freshly ground black pepper

1. *Grits*: In a medium saucepan, bring water and vegan butter to a boil. Stir in the grits, salt the water, return to a boil, and reduce the heat to a simmer for 10 minutes or until the grits are thick and have absorbed most of the water, stirring occasionally to prevent the grits from sticking. Add the soy milk, 1/2 cup at a time, and cook, stirring occasionally, until the liquid is absorbed and the desired consistency is reached: very creamy but full-bodied enough to hold its shape, about 50 minutes. Stir in remaining ingredients and keep warm.

2. *Greens:* In a large skillet or wok, heat olive oil over medium-high heat. Add kale and salt and cook, stirring frequently, for about 5 minutes. Add water and cook, still stirring frequently, for 5 minutes or until kale is softened and cooked down a little, but still bright green. Stir in vinegar and syrup. Taste and adjust seasoning if necessary.

3. *Gravy:* Heat the oil in a large skillet over medium-high heat. Add the onion and sauté until softened, 3 to 5 minutes. Add the mushrooms and sauté 2 minutes. Add the rosemary and continue to sauté and stir the mushrooms until most of their moisture has been released and cooked off and they begin to turn golden.

4. In a food processor, combine the beans, vegetable stock, and garlic, and blend until smooth, scraping down the sides of the bowl as necessary. Once the mushrooms are golden, stir in the bean mixture and cook, stirring, for 2 minutes. Season with sherry, lemon juice, nutmeg, and salt and pepper to taste, stirring to combine.

5. To serve, arrange the greens on a platter or in a shallow bowl, spoon the grits on top and top with the gravy. Sprinkle with nuts, if using. Serve hot.

pears foster french toast

Yield: 4 servings

In this delicious dish, I substitute pears for bananas to take advantage of one of winter's gifts. If you're a little fire phobic like me, you can enjoy this classic flambéed dessert without the pyrotechnics.

French Toast:
8 (1-inch thick) bias-cut slices French bread (from a long baguette)
4 ounces firm silken tofu
3/4 cup soy milk
2 tablespoons chickpea flour
2 tablespoons maple syrup
1/2 teaspoon vanilla extract
1/4 teaspoon pumpkin pie spice (or ground cinnamon)

Pinch sea salt

Topping:
4 tablespoons vegan butter
4 tablespoons brown sugar
2 pears, halved, cored, cut into 1/8-inch slices and cut crosswise into thirds
1/4 teaspoon sea salt
2 tablespoons cornstarch
2 tablespoons cool water
2 teaspoons fresh lemon juice or to taste

1. *French Toast:* Preheat the oven to 350°F. If bread is fresh, dry it out by placing on a baking pan in the oven for 3 to 5 minutes. Combine all the remaining ingredients in a food processor or blender. Process until smooth, scraping down sides of bowl as needed. Pour the mixture into a small bowl and dip each slice of bread into the mixture on both sides. Transfer to a plate, then repeat, dipping the bread in the mixture again on both sides. Set aside.

2. *Topping:* In a large skillet over medium-high heat, melt the vegan butter. Add the brown sugar and stir until melted. Add the pears and a pinch of salt and sauté for 3 minutes. Whisk together the cornstarch and water in a small bowl until completely combined and add to pears, cooking and stirring for 2 minutes. Remove from the heat, add the lemon juice, and stir to combine well.

3. *To assemble:* Flip and dip the bread again, and transfer to a well oiled shallow baking dish or heatproof skillet. Spoon the topping around and over the bread. Bake for about 30 minutes, checking after 20 and 25 minutes, or until bread is set and the exposed surfaces are golden brown.

baked asian pears stuffed with streusel-topped rice pudding

Yield: 4 servings

A gift of a big locally-grown Asian pear gave rise to this homey morning treat. This dish will lure you out of bed even on the most frigid of winter mornings.

Pears:
2 large round Asian pears
2 teaspoons maple syrup

Rice Pudding:
1 cup cooked brown rice
1 cup soy milk
4 tablespoons natural sugar
1/4 teaspoon almond extract

2 teaspoons lemon zest

Streusel:
2 tablespoons old-fashioned oatmeal
1 tablespoon natural sugar
1 tablespoon coarsely chopped pecans
1 teaspoon canola oil

To assemble:
4 tablespoons soy creamer

1. **Pears:** Preheat the oven to 400°F. Spray a small baking dish with nonstick spray. Halve the pears lengthwise, and scoop out the cores to leave golf-ball size hollows for the stuffing. Cut a thin slice from the rounded sides to create a flat surface so the pear halves don't wobble.

2. Arrange the pears, cut-side up, in the prepared baking dish and bake 15 to 25 minutes or until they are crisp tender when pierced with a knife. Brush each pear half with 1/2 teaspoon maple syrup and bake 5 minutes longer. Remove from the oven and set aside.

3. **Rice Pudding:** In a saucepan, combine the rice, soy milk, and sugar, and heat to a simmer over medium-high heat. Cook, stirring frequently, until all of liquid is absorbed, 5 to 7 minutes. Remove the pan from the heat. Stir in the almond extract and lemon zest. Set aside.

4. **Streusel:** Spray an 8-inch baking pan with nonstick spray. In a small bowl, combine all streusel ingredients until well mixed. Sprinkle the streusel into the pan and bake for about 10 minutes, stirring several times and watching closely so it doesn't burn.

5. **To assemble:** Spoon the rice pudding into each pear half. To serve, arrange each stuffed pear in a shallow bowl or individual gratin dish. Pour a tablespoon of soy creamer over each pear half, and garnish each with a tablespoon of the streusel. Serve immediately.

Acknowledgments

Like all cookbooks, this one is the result of a lifetime of involvement with food. Food is highly personal, political, practical, and poetic; it encompasses all. So the inspiration that has directly shaped this book has come from virtually everywhere; certainly from far too many sources to adequately credit, including a host of authors, bloggers, chefs, and home cooks, both vegan and non. These talented individuals have greatly expanded my understanding of food and my appreciation for the people who prepare and eat it. I bow in the direction of each and every one.

A few of those inspired and inspiring home cooks, so central to the formation of my own ideas about food, are family members: especially my parents, Byron and Sallie Gough; and also my mother-in-law, Terry DiJulio, and my late father-in-law, Tony DiJulio; my aunts and uncles, Bessie and Earl Weed, Jr., and Jo and Wally White; both of my late grandmothers, Cammie Jackson and Virginia White; my sister, sisters-in-law and brother-in-law, Ginny Gough, Tina DiJulio, and Terri and David Lindelow; and my cooking cousins, especially Earl Weed, III. I am grateful to my clan for the joy of living contentedly bound to them by blood and by marriage at the confluence of familial culinary traditions that are as unique as they are universal.

Among the other gifted cooks who have been particularly influential in my culinary life are my dear friends Yvette Hetrick, Monica Holmes, Trish Pfeifer, Allison Price and Donna Reiss. Innumerable ideas from our conversations and our shared experiences of food and much more have found their way into the pages of this book. I thank them for that and for their abiding friendships without which existence would be intolerably bland. A host of additional friends, relatives – especially my husband, Joe – students, colleagues, and blog followers have served as tasters and, whether wittingly or unwittingly, as catalysts for the development of my culinary traditions and innovations. I am obliged to them all for teaching me to savor what is important.

The opportunity to write this cookbook – to hone and to share my culinary point of view and to discover more about food, life, and myself through the work – is one of the greatest gifts anyone could give me. The whole experience feels almost like an embarrassment of riches. To say that I am grateful to the giver of that gift, my editor and publisher Jon Robertson of the Vegan Heritage Press, does not begin to describe the depth of my appreciation. A quote from one of my most cherished books, *The Heart of Darkness*, is especially appropriate: "I tell you...this man has enlarged my mind." Throughout this process, Jon has been the knowledgeable, wise, gracious, and unfailingly patient professor; me the "hungry" student. He had his work cut out for him, but he approached it with warmth, wit, and compassion, always inviting my questions – a potentially risky proposition with me. Ultimately, he somehow made me feel that this book is entirely my creation, yet simultaneously the result of a dynamic and symbiotic partnership. I thank him for his vision, his trust, and his steadfastness. And to his wife Robin, a prolific vegan cookbook author, freelance food writer, and blogger in her own right, I offer my appreciation for her encouragement and advice from the perspective of someone who has "been there." Thanks also to the editors, designers, and staff of Vegan Heritage Press."

Betsy DiJulio

About the Author

A vegan blogger, freelance writer, and food stylist, Betsy DiJulio wrote "The Veggie Table" column for Norfolk, VA's *Virginian-Pilot* newspaper. A lifetime cooking enthusiast, Betsy has worked as a caterer, taught private cooking classes in Hampton Roads Virginia, and has won national recipe competitions. As a writer, DiJulio focuses on topics of vegan and organic food, art, home and garden design, and green initiatives.

A practicing artist, Betsy DiJulio, M.A., Ed.S., is a full-time art teacher at Princess Anne High School in the Virginia Beach (VA) City Public Schools, where she was chosen as the 2010 Citywide Teacher of the Year. Since 2002, she has been the official artist for the San Diego-based Competitors Group's "Rock 'n' Roll Half Marathon" in Virginia Beach.

This longtime vegetarian-turned-vegan is an animal lover, animal rights supporter, and Virginia Beach SPCA volunteer. DiJulio and her husband, Joe, have been married since 1990 and share their home with a pack of beloved canines. See Betsy's website at www.TheBloomingPlatter.com.

Index

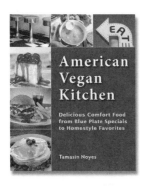

American Vegan Kitchen

Delicious Comfort Food from Blue Plate Specials to Homestyle Favorites

Tamasin Noyes

Do you ever crave the delicious comfort foods served at your local diner, deli, or neighborhood cafe? This cookbook shows you how to make vegan versions of your favorite dishes in your own home kitchen.

These 200+ recipes will satisfy vegans and non-vegans alike with deli sandwiches, burgers and fries, mac and cheese, pasta, pizza, omelets, pancakes, soups and salads, casseroles, and desserts. Enjoy truly great American flavors from tempting ethnic dishes to the homestyle comfort foods of the heartland.

From coast-to-coast and cover-to-cover, *American Vegan Kitchen* helps you serve up great homestyle vegan recipes for breakfast, lunch, dinner, and desserts. The book contains eight pages of full-color photos and helpful icons to bring American comfort food home to your table.

See Tami's blog at: www.veganappetite.com.

Vegan Heritage Press
Paperback, 232 pages,
ISBN: 978-0-9800131-1-5
$18.95, 7½" x 9"

Vegan Unplugged

How to Eat Well When the Power Goes Out

by Jon Robertson with recipes by Robin Robertson

Vegan Unplugged is your go-to source for gourmet pantry cooking in a variety of worst-case scenarios. Make tasty meals whenever the power goes out from storms, hurricanes, and blackouts. These recipes are quick and easy, and can be made in fifteen minutes or less. This makes the book ideal for camping, boating, or anytime you just don't feel like cooking.

Vegan Unplugged provides easy, practical tips on how to shop for, store, and quickly prepare nonperishable pantry foods. Make great dishes such as Almost-Instant Black Bean Chili, Pantry Pasta Salad, Fire-Roasted Blueberry Cobbler, and more. This book is a "must have" for anyone who wants to be ready for anything with great-tasting, nutritious pantry cuisine.

See Jon's blog: http://veganunplugged.blogspot.com.

Vegan Heritage Press
Paperback, 216 pages,
ISBN: 978-0-9800131-2-2
$14.95, 7½" x 7½"